Student Workbook

Light to the Nations II:
The Making of the Modern World

Contributors to the Workbook:
Katherine S. Zehnder
Ana Braga-Henebry, MA

General Editor: Christopher J. Zehnder, MA

Catholic Textbook Project

Table of Contents

Introduction: The Scientific Revolution

1. *Answer the following. (pgs. 1-5)*

a. Describe the culture of the Middle Ages. _____

_____

_____

b. When did the Renaissance begin? _____

c. How did the Renaissance change Medieval culture? _____

_____

_____

_____

d. What ended the Renaissance? _____

e. Why was the period that followed the Renaissance called the "scientific revolution"? _____

_____

_____

_____

f. Did people in the 16th and 17th centuries make a distinction between *science* and *philosophy*? Why or why not?

_____

_____

_____

g. What Greek philosopher influenced the thought of the Middle Ages? _____

h. According to this philosopher, what are the beginnings or principles of all knowledge? _____

_____

i. What method of reasoning did Medieval philosophers use? _____

j. Describe this method of reasoning. _____

_____

_____

_____

_____

k. Name **two** famous Medieval theologians who used this method of reasoning.

_____   _____

l. What is an experiment? _____

_____

_____

_____

m. Can the experimental method tell us everything we need or want to know? Explain. _____

_____

_____

_____

n. How are the methods of deduction and experiment similar? How do they differ? _____

_____

_____

_____

_____

o. Why did 16th century thinkers begin to think that experimental science was the only way to come to definite knowledge about the world? _____

_____

_____

_____

2. *Match the columns. (pgs. 5 – 6)*

A. Copernicus   [   ] Greek astronomer who taught that the earth was at the center of the universe

B. heliocentric   [   ] work that explains how the heavenly bodies move around the sun

C. Ptolemy   [   ] Polish astronomer who taught that the sun was at the center of the universe.

D. *Almagest*   [   ] earth centered

E. geocentric   [   ] sun centered

F. *On the Revolution of the Heavenly Spheres*   [   ] work that explains the motion of the heavenly bodies using complicated mathematics and ingenious explanations

3. Explain why the Copernican theory was considered revolutionary. *(pg. 6)*

_____

_____

_____

_____

_____

Name _____ Date _____

4. *Answer the following. (pg. 7)*

a. What is a hypothesis? Give an example of a hypothesis. _____

_____

_____

b. How does a hypothesis become more certain? _____

_____

_____

5. Write a brief biography of Galileo. Include his discoveries and famous invention. *(pgs. 7 – 8)*

6. *Answer the following. (pgs. 9 – 12)*

a. What hypothesis did Galileo assert as truth? _____

_____

b. Since the Church is not an of enemy of science, why did it oppose Galileo's idea? Give **two** reasons.

_____

_____

_____

_____

c. What did the Holy Office of the Inquisition forbid Galileo to do? _____

_____

_____

d. What did Galileo do in response to the Holy Office's decree?

_____

_____

e. What change had to be made before Copernicus's *On the Revolution of the Heavenly Spheres* could be published?

_____

_____

f. What did the new pope, Urban VIII, allow Galileo to do? _____

_____

_____

g. Why was Galileo called to trial before the Holy Office in 1633? _____

_____

_____

_____

h. What did the Holy Office declare on June 23, 1633 at the end of the trial? _____

_____

_____

i. What was Galileo's sentence? _____

_____

_____

j. Despite this sentence, did Galileo give up his views? _____

_____

k. How did Galileo spend the remaining years of his life? _____

_____

_____

l. Because of the trial of Galileo, what have people accused the Church of? _____

_____

_____

m. Why is this accusation false and unhistorical? _____

_____

_____

_____

_____

Did you know? The director of the Vatican Observatory is Fr. Guy Consolmagno, a Jesuit priest and an American astronomer. His book *Turn Left at Orion* is a popular book for beginning astronomers. See if you can discover more about "The Pope's Astronomer."

7. *Fill in the blank with the correct name. (pg. 8, pgs. 12-14)*

a. _____ was a Danish astronomer who rejected the Copernican theory. He discovered a *nova stella* in the constellation Cassiopeia, and spent his life observing and cataloging the stars from his observatory built by King II of Denmark.

b. _____ was a German astronomer who accepted the Copernican theory, but through his observations concluded that the planets do not move in perfect circles around the sun, but in elliptical paths or patterns. He called these patterns "laws" and believed that these laws showed order in the universe and the power and wisdom of God.

c. _____ was a second century Greek physician whose theories on medicine and physiology were definitive for Europeans and Arabs until the 1600s.

d. _____ was a 17th century English scientists who discovered how blood circulates in the human body.

e. _____ was an ex-politician who devoted himself to philosophy. He thought all Medieval philosophy should be swept away and replaced with philosophy that is based on experiment alone.

8. *Match the columns. (pg. 14)*

A. induction   [   ] theory that truth can only be found though experience and experiment

B. rationalism   [   ] method which begins with a hypothesis that is tested through repeated experiments

C. empiricism   [   ] theory that truth can be known and problems solved only by human reason and experience

9. *Underline the phrases that describes Francis Bacon's new philosophy. (pgs. 13 – 14)*

Respected Aristotelean logic.   Knowledge should be sought because it is good in itself.

Thought deduction was utterly useless.   Nature should be studied to control nature.

The ultimate purpose of knowledge is to know God.   True knowledge comes only through experiment.

Only practical knowledge is important.   Inspiration and faith are valid paths to truth.

Reason and faith can contradict each other.   Knowledge should be sought only for power.

Influenced modern scientific thought.   Denied the existence of God.

10. Finish this quote from Sir Francis Bacon. *(pg. 13)*

"Knowledge itself is _____"

11. What did you learn about Sir Isaac Newton? *Complete the following. (pgs. 15-18)*

a. Write four words or phrases that describe Sir Isaac Newton.

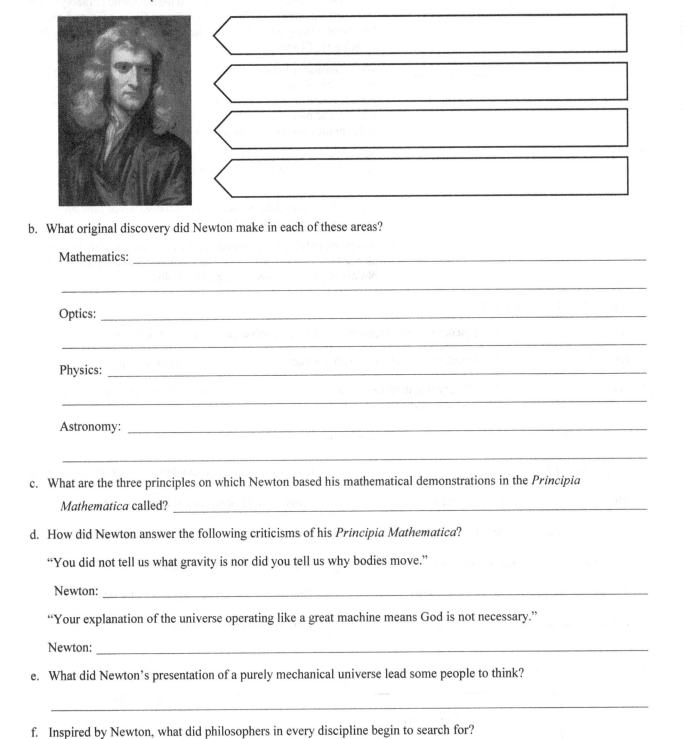

b. What original discovery did Newton make in each of these areas?

Mathematics: _____

_____

Optics: _____

_____

Physics: _____

_____

Astronomy: _____

_____

c. What are the three principles on which Newton based his mathematical demonstrations in the *Principia*

Mathematica called? _____

d. How did Newton answer the following criticisms of his *Principia Mathematica*?

"You did not tell us what gravity is nor did you tell us why bodies move."

Newton: _____

"Your explanation of the universe operating like a great machine means God is not necessary."

Newton: _____

e. What did Newton's presentation of a purely mechanical universe lead some people to think?

_____

f. Inspired by Newton, what did philosophers in every discipline begin to search for?

_____

Name _____ Date _____

Chapter 1: **The Age of Enlightenment**

1. *Answer the following. (pgs. 21 – 23)*

a. What subject interested René Descartes the most? _____

b. What were the two questions that troubled Descartes while he was studying philosophy?

  _____

  _____

c. After contemplation and prayer, what was the "light" he discovered that answered his questions?

  _____

  _____

d. Give the name of the book Descartes wrote that developed his new philosophical ideas.

  _____

e. Complete these ideas that are found in Descartes's book:

> I must realize that everything I think I know is nothing but _____ I learned as a child.
>
> I must _____ anything and everything I think I know.
>
> I escape _____ by realizing that only a _____ being can _____.
>
> If I am a _____ being, I must also _____ because if I didn't _____,
>
> I couldn't _____!

f. Finish Descartes's famous phrase that sums up his philosophy. Write it in Latin and English.

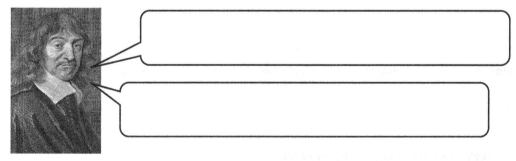

Did you know? Descartes is also famous for developing analytic or Cartesian geometry. His use of a horizontal X-axis and vertical Y-axis explained geometry in algebraic terms. His grid became the basis for calculus. "Cartesian" comes from Descartes's name in Latin.

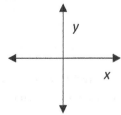

g. Complete Descartes's ideas about God:

> Where does my thought of God, a perfectly _____ being, come from?
>
> It cannot come from me because I am not perfectly _____.
>
> The idea of God must come from _____ himself.
>
> Therefore, God must _____!
>
> Since God is perfectly _____, he would not _____ or deceive me.
>
> Therefore, everything in the world I can sense must also _____.

h. Complete more of Descartes's ideas:

> The material world and the human body operate according to fixed and eternal _____ that cannot be changed.
>
> The material world is like a vast _____.
>
> _____ set the world in motion, but then left it to run on its own without any further help.
>
> Since the human _____ is not material, it is the only thing in the world that is _____.

i.   What Catholic beliefs did Descartes's philosophy undermine? _____
_____
_____

j.   What **two** modern doctrines did Descartes's ideas encourage?

_____   _____

k.   Did Descartes wish to encourage these ideas? _____

l.   Did the Catholic Church reject or accept Descartes's philosophy? _____

2. *Answer the following. (pgs. 23 – 24)*

a.   What is skepticism? _____
_____

b.   What were some other causes of skepticism in the 17th century besides Descartes's philosophy? *Give **two** causes.*

   • _____

   • _____

c.   Libertines or "freethinkers" wanted freedom in what **two** areas of life?

   ✓ _____

   ✓ _____

Did you know? Libertine comes from the Latin word *liber* which means "free." Skeptic comes from the Greek word *skepsis or skeptikos* which means doubt or question.

3. *Answer the following. (pgs. 24 – 25)*

a. What was the new religion that developed from rationalism? _____

b. Put a check mark next to the sentences that describe this new religion:

_____ God intervenes in the affairs of the world and cares for his creation.

_____ God set the universe in motion and left it alone to continue by the laws of nature.

_____ God is a spiritual being utterly separate from the universe he created.

_____ It is useless and irrational to pray to God.

_____ Reason must judge religion as well as science.

_____ Jesus Christ is God, the second person of the Trinity.

_____ Belief in the Trinity, the Incarnation, the Resurrection, and miracles are irrational.

_____ Jesus Christ is a great ethical teacher, but not God.

_____ We know how we ought to behave because God has revealed the moral law to mankind.

_____ Humans should behave in any way they want.

_____ Humans learn how they ought to behave by using their reason alone.

_____ Religion should require people to attend church to worship God.

_____ Religion should only require people to lead moral lives.

_____ The Christian Faith should be outlawed.

_____ Christianity is not true, but it is useful in controlling uneducated people.

_____ Only educated freethinkers can be members of the new religion.

c. Name **three** shocking claims made by the philosopher Spinoza in his *Theological-Political Treatise*:

- _____

- _____

- _____

d. Complete Spinoza's radical ideas found in *Demonstrated in the Manner of Geometry*:

The mind (or soul) _____, so it is not _____.

The mind and all matter are _____ thing and that is _____.

Therefore, the natural laws by which the universe runs are the _____ of _____.

e. Who is known as the "Father of the Enlightenment"? _____

f. What was the name of his influential work? _____

g. Describe this work and why it was a powerful tool in spreading skepticism: _____

_____

_____

_____

_____

_____

4. Complete this paragraph about the philosopher Thomas Hobbes and his ideas: *(pgs. 27 -28)*

In 1651 Hobbes published a book called _____

or the Matter, Form, and Power of a Commonwealth, Ecclesiastical and Civil.

The title refers to a creature of the _____, a fearsome

_____ that lives in the depths of the sea. In this book Hobbes

presents a very _____ view of human nature. He thought a

human being was merely a kind of _____ without an

immaterial _____ or a free _____. Left to themselves,

people will do only what _____ them without thinking about _____. Hobbes said that

originally humans lived in a "state of _____" where they knew nothing about _____ or

_____, justice or _____. In this state, life was a _____ of every man against

every _____. To escape this terrible situation, people banded together to form a _____.

They made a "social _____" with a sovereign _____ who would provide peace and

_____ if they gave up all their _____. The _____ had absolute

_____ over his subjects and could not be disobeyed. According to Hobbes, _____ is the

servant of the government and must help keep order. Hobbes concluded that the _____ is the "great

_____" that must control everything. Hobbes's radical book influenced some of the leading

_____ of the late 17th century.

5. Complete this paragraph about the philosopher John Locke and his ideas. *(pgs. 28 – 29)*

In 1690 John Locke published his most important work – *Two* _____.

Locke's ideas about the "state of _____" were similar to Hobbes's, but Locke did not think humans were

always cruel and _____. He thought humans followed a _____ law (the _____

law) that required them to respect the _____ of others. He said there were three _____ that no

one could justly take away from people and those were _____, _____, and _____.

When people formed their social _____ they gave up only some of their _____, not their

three inalienable ones. The people could _____ their government if it violated the _____

of individuals and _____ a new one in its place. Locke's ideas provided a theory of

_____ that has become the basis of most _____ thinking from his time to our own.

6. *Answer the following. (pg. 29)*

a. According to Locke, what was the most important individual right and what is its definition?

_____

_____

b. According to Locke, what form of government is the most likely to protect this right?

_____

Name _____ Date _____

7. *Finish these sentences: (pgs. 29 – 30)*

a. Liberalism is a political and social philosophy that _____

_____

b. To the Liberal way of thinking, human beings by nature are _____

_____

c. To the Liberal thinker, government exists to _____

_____

d. According to Liberalism, individuals first and foremost _____

e. According to Liberalism, the function of government is to make sure _____

_____

8. *Read the statements below. If a statement describes a Liberal attitude, write a "L" on the line. If it describes a Medieval Catholic attitude, write a "M" on the line. (pgs. 29 – 30)*

a. ____ Human beings are made by God to live in society with others.

b. ____ Human beings by nature are individuals who live without connection to anyone

c. ____ Only in society can people attain the common good.

d. ____ The greatest good is everlasting union with God in heaven.

e. ____ The greatest good is individual liberty.

f. ____ Government exists only to keep individuals from hurting one another.

g. ____ Government is a necessary evil – if we could live without it, we would.

h. ____ Government is natural to man and it helps men achieve the common good.

i. ____ Government should fight immorality and heresy and promote the true religion.

j. ____ Religion is private opinion and government should not promote one religion over another.

k. ____ Individuals should be permitted to speak and to publish their opinions, no matter what they are.

l. ____ Individuals should not be permitted to speak and publish opinions which destroy the common good.

9. Review: *Match the columns.*

A. Descartes   [   ] man in the state of nature is nasty and brutal

B. Divine Providence   [   ] one who wants freedom of thought and morals

C. skepticism   [   ] God keeps the world in existence and cares for his creation

D. libertine   [   ] society is directed toward the freedom of individuals, not the common good

E. Deism   [   ] Locke's inalienable rights of man

F. Spinoza   [   ] "I think, therefore I am."

G. Hobbes   [   ] father of political Liberalism

H. life, liberty, property   [   ] nothing can be known for certain to be true

I. Locke   [   ] the universe is God

J. Liberalism   [   ] the religious side of rationalism

10. Fill in the blanks to complete this story of Voltaire's early life. *(pgs. 31 – 33)*

Voltaire was a _____ class Frenchman who mixed with aristocratic _____ and attended Paris _____ where _____ and irreligious ideas were discussed. When he was a young man, he was imprisoned in the _____ for writing poems _____ the French regent. After his release Voltaire earned fame as a _____. He not only had a successful literary career, he also became a very _____ man through financial _____, investments, and making friends with _____. However, his bitter and sarcastic _____ got him into trouble and he again found himself in the _____. He was then sent from France to _____ for three years. While in that country, Voltaire discovered the works of the scientist _____ and the philosopher _____ and became a great admirer of _____ society. He returned to France as a _____ and wrote commentaries on _____ and works against _____. He attacked the French _____ and state. To escape arrest, Voltaire fled to the independent duchy of _____. In his new home, he performed _____ and wrote more and more about _____, philosophy, and _____. His writings made _____ ideas more popular. He had a clear, _____, and _____ style of writing. His cruel _____ made his opponents' ideas seem _____. He told outright _____ to promote his ideas and destroy those of others. He rejected all traditional _____ as foolish and superstitious. He denied the immortality of the _____ and was a proponent of _____ libertinism. His chief enemy (which he called "the _____ one") was the _____ _____. He accused it of pretending it was the one, true _____ just to fool and _____ the masses. He thought _____ might be fine for ignorant, common people, but educated men should look to _____ and _____ for guidance on how to live. He became the greatest advocate of _____ tolerance in the 18th century. Since he thought the common man could never be "enlightened", he opposed _____ and favored a government run by an "enlightened" and absolute _____. Voltaire's use of the term "_____" gave the name to 18th century movement toward Liberal ideas.

11. What was Diderot's *Encyclopedia*? Why was it instrumental in undermining religion and tradition? *(pgs. 33 – 34)*

_____

_____

_____

_____

_____

_____

Name _____ Date _____

12. *Answer the following. (pgs. 34 – 37)*

a. Despite his own troubled life and moral failures, what conclusion did Rousseau come to about human beings?

_____

b. What did Rousseau think about Society? _____

_____

c. In his first published work, what did Rousseau say was the ideal life for humans?

_____

d. In his second work, what did Rousseau say was the ideal life or life in the "state of nature"?

_____

e. What did Rousseau think was the cause of societal corruption and oppression?

_____

f. What did Rousseau think was the solution to society's problems? _____

_____

_____

_____

g. What did Rousseau think about religion? _____

_____

h. What three religious doctrines did Rousseau think all should believe?

- _____

- _____

- _____

i. What was Rousseau's attitude about the Catholic Faith? _____

_____

j. What was Rousseau's most important and influential published work? _____

k. Complete his ideas expressed in his book:

> The authority of the state comes from the combined will of the _____.

> The sovereign power does not belong to _____, but to the _____.

> To preserve their _____ and _____, individuals join together and make a _____ contract with each other.

> In this contract they lose their _____ and agree to be ruled by the " _____ _____ " of all.

l. What was Rousseau's ideal form of government? _____

m. What movement did Rousseau's ideas inspire? _____

n. What did Voltaire think about Rousseau's ideas? _____

_____

_____

Dig Deeper: Have you ever heard someone say something like, "He was philosophical about his job loss." In such a sentence "philosophical" means calm, realistic, or reasonable. The implication is that if you use your reason, you'll remain calm about your problems and your happiness will not be disturbed. Do you think the modern philosophers Voltaire and Rousseau were happy men? Why or why not? Were the medieval philosophers Albert the Great and Thomas Aquinas happy men? What contributed to their happiness or unhappiness? Write your thoughts below.

Chapter 2: The Age of Enlightened Despots

1. Write four words or phrases that describe Pyotr Alexeievich Romanov: *(pgs. 41 – 45)*

2. What were Pyotr's **two** goals for Russia? *(pg. 41)*

- _____

- _____

3. *Answer the following: (pgs. 42 – 43)*

a. What were the eastern and western borders of the vast Russian Empire under Tsar Pyotr?

_____

b. Why were the Russians such avid pioneers? _____

_____

c. Fill in this pyramid to illustrate the structure of Russian society under Tsar Pyotr:

d. How did Russian life and culture differ from western European culture? _____

_____

_____

_____

e. What did western Europeans think about Russia? _____

_____

After reading the explanation on Russian names on pg. 43, figure out what your name would be if you lived in Russia:

4. *Fill in the blanks. (pgs. 43 – 44)*

a. To find out more about western European industry and crafts, Pytor travelled throughout Europe disguised as a simple _____.

b. Pyotr conquered the Turkish city of _____ so Russia could have a _____ port on the Black Sea to carry on _____ year-round.

c. Pyotr's manner of handling rebellion showed the Russian people that he would _____ to accomplish his goals.

d. To make sure nothing stood in the way of _____ Russia, Pytor built a large standing _____.

e. In order to control the Russian Orthodox Church, Pytor refused to appoint a new _____ and gave authority over the Church to the _____ which was headed by a _____ chosen by the tsar.

f. Pytor weakened the power and influence of the _____ by creating new families of nobility who would faithful to him alone.

5. *Complete the following. (pgs. 44 – 45)*

a. Give **four** examples of how Pyotr forced the Russians to be like western Europeans:

- _____
- _____
- _____
- _____

b. Give **four** examples of Pyotr acting "like a father" towards his subjects:

- _____
- _____
- _____
- _____

6. Complete these facts about the Great Northern War: *(pgs. 45 – 46)*

a. Who: _____

b. Why: _____

c. When: _____

d. Where: _____

e. Outcome: _____

_____

7. Why is Tsar Pyotr I called "the Great"? _____

_____

_____

_____

8. *Answer the following. (pgs. 47 – 48)*

a. What ideas influenced Katerina the Great? _____

_____

b. How did Katerina make Russian aristocrats cultured and "enlightened"?

_____

_____

c. What "enlightened" projects did Katerina initiate in Russia?

_____

_____

d. How did Katerina treat the Russian Church? _____

_____

e. What was the life of the poor like under Katerina's rule? _____

_____

f. Why is Katerina called "the Great"? _____

_____

_____

Review: *Match the columns. (pgs. 41 – 48)*

A. Moscow   [   ] traditional Russia that lived on in the monks and peasants

B. "Germans"   [   ] traditional ruling assembly of Russia

C. serfs   [   ] range that runs north to south, dividing Europe from Asia

D. Azov   [   ] traditional capital city of Russia

E. Ural Mountains   [   ] title of a female ruler of Russia

F. tsar   [   ] Swedish army destroyed a vastly larger Russian army

G. Arkhangelsk   [   ] German princess married to Pyotr III; i.e. Katerina the Great

H. boyars   [   ] what the Russians called all western Europeans

I. Great Northern War   [   ] Russia's first warm-water port

J. Karl XII   [   ] workers bound to live and work a piece of land

K. Battle of Narva   [   ] Russia's northern port on the White Sea

L. St. Petersburg   [   ] title of a male ruler of Russia

M. tsarina   [   ] young brilliant military leader of Sweden

N. Sophia Augusta Frederica   [   ] highest aristocrats in Russia

O. Holy Mother Russia   [   ] new capital city of Russia on the Baltic Sea

P. duma   [   ] 21-year struggle between Russia and Sweden for control of the Baltic

9. Russia occupies two continents – Europe and Asia. Most of the events in Russia's history have occurred on the European (western) side. *Follow the instructions, using the map of western Russia below.*
(Refer to maps on pgs. 42 and 46 in your textbook.)

a. Outline the western boundary of Russia.
b. Label: **Volga River, Black Sea, Baltic Sea**
c. Label the countries: **Russia, Sweden, Poland**
d. Label the ports: **Azov, Arkhangelsk**
e. Label the cities: **Moscow, St. Petersburg**
f. Underline the city that was the traditional capitol of Russia.
g. Circle the city that Pyotr built for his new capital.
h. As you can see from the map on page 51 in your textbook, **Prussia** is in the area below the Baltic Sea. Label it.

Did you know? "Russia" and "Prussia" sound very similar and you might think they are related, but they are not. Russia was named after the Nordic or Viking tribe – the Rus – which settled western Russia. Prussia comes from the German word "Preussen" – the name of a Baltic people that occupied the area and were conquered by the Germans.

10. Fill in the blanks to complete the story of Prussia. *(pgs. 48 – 50)*

The Kingdom of Prussia developed from duchies controlled by the German

_____ family. In 1701 the _____ _____ Emperor

allowed the ruler of these areas to call himself "king" in exchange for his help in a war

against _____. Thus, Elector _____ Hohenzollern became King

_____ and named his whole kingdom Prussia. Prussia was a _____

kingdom, but it became a great power under its second king, Friedrich _____ I.

By being frugal and living simply, Friedrich _____ saved _____

and filled his _____. He built up a large _____, made up of both nobles and _____.

Ruthless _____ and capable officers made the Prussian _____ one of the most effective

_____ forces in Europe. Yet, the king used his _____ mainly for defense, and he did not neglect

the other needs of his kingdom. He established a _____ _____ bureaucracy to regulate the

_____ and encourage _____ and industry. He issued an edict forbidding the _____

to seize peasant-owned _____. He established village _____ throughout Prussia and decreed that

every _____ in his dominion must attend. Despite the good he did, the king was feared because of his violent

_____. He thought _____ was necessary in disciplining soldiers and even his own

_____.

Name _____ Date _____

11. *Answer the following. (pg. 50 – 52)*

a. Describe the education of the Crown Prince Friedrich (Fritz):

Parlez-vous Francais?

_____

_____

_____

b. In what ways was Fritz the opposite of his father? _____

_____

_____

c. Why did Fritz's father hate the French? _____

_____

d. Why was the young Fritz a disappointment to his father? _____

_____

e. How did the king treat Fritz? _____

_____

_____

f. How were Fritz and his father finally reconciled? _____

_____

_____

_____

_____

g. What were some of Fritz's interests during the "happiest years" of his life at Rheinsberg?

_____

_____

h. Who was biggest influence on Fritz's political ideas? _____

i. Explain Fritz's ideas expressed in his book *The Anti-Machiavelli:* _____

_____

_____

_____

j. What advice did the dying king give to Fritz about war? _____

_____

k. What was Fritz's official title when he was crowned king after his father's death?

_____

12. *Fill in the blanks. (pgs. 53 – 54)*

By the late 17th century the German empire, called the _____ covered a vast area of central Europe, but lacked _____. The _____ had allowed every prince to choose the _____ he wanted his people to follow, so the empire was divided into _____ and Protestant regions. The emperor was elected from the powerful _____ family, but he had little or no power over the 300 states that made up the empire. The _____ had ruined Germany. The German _____ lived in dire poverty made worse by heavy tax burdens. _____ became the most powerful and prosperous German state in the late 17th century. The ambitious _____ family gained other lands outside the empire which absorbed their attention and caused them to further _____ the empire. It was difficult to rule domains with so many different _____. By the end of Emperor _____'s reign, the empire was smaller with a weakened and disorganized _____.

13. *Match the columns (pgs. 54 – 56)*

A. Pragmatic Sanction	[ ] ally of Prussia, enemy of Great Britain
B. Maria Theresia	[ ] elector of Bavaria and ally of Prussia
C. Fritz van Hohenzollern	[ ] ally of Austria, enemy of France
D. Silesia	[ ] land of the Magyars; ally of Austria against Prussia
E. Karl Albrecht	[ ] Archduchess of Austria and queen of Bohemia and Hungary
F. Franz of Lorraine	[ ] husband of Maria Theresia; crowned Holy Roman Emperor in 1745
G. France	[ ] ally of Prussia, enemy of Great Britain
H. Hungary	[ ] King Friedrich II of Prussia
I. Great Britain	[ ] duchy between Brandenburg and Bohemia, conquered by Prussia
J. Spain	[ ] decree that allowed a Habsburg ruler to pass down his lands to his daughter if there was no son to succeed him

14. *Answer the following. (pgs. 56 – 57)*

a. What action ignited the war between Austria and Prussia? _____

_____

b. What agreement was ignored when taking this action and why did Prussia feel confident in taking this step?

_____

_____

c. What was the outcome of the War of the Austrian Succession? _____

_____

_____

Name _____ Date _____

15. *Answer the following. (pgs. 57 – 58)*

a. What is a despot? _____

b. What is an "enlightened despot"? _____

_____

c. Give **five** characteristics of Voltaire's ideal ruler:

- _____

- _____

- _____

- _____

- _____

d. In what way was Friedrich the Great a despot? _____

_____

e. Give **two** ways Friedrich the Great was like his father: _____

_____

f. How was Friedrich the Great's attitude about war different from his father's? _____

_____

g. Give **four** examples to show how Friedrich the Great improved life in Prussia:

- _____

- _____

- _____

- _____

h. In what ways was Friedrich's attitude toward religion the same as Voltaire's?

_____

_____

_____

_____

i. Complete Friedrich's quote about religion:

"All religions must be _____ and every person

_____ "

16. *Answer the following. (pgs. 59 – 60)*

a. Why did Maria Theresia begin reforms in her domains?

_____

_____

b. Give **three** of Maria Theresia's reforms:

- _____

- _____

- _____

c. Why did Maria Theresia form an alliance against Prussia? _____

_____

d. What countries were Maria Theresia's main allies? _____

e. What country was Friedrich's main ally?_____

f. What action started the Seven Years' War? _____

_____

g. What war was being fought in North American at the same time as the Seven Years' War and what were the two countries that were fighting?

_____

h. Why was the Seven Years' War the first world war in history? _____

_____

_____

i. When did the Seven Years' War end? _____

j. What did Prussia gain in the Treaty of Hubertusburg? _____

k. Why was the Seven Years' War important for Prussia? _____

_____

_____

l. What lands did Great Britain gain in the Peace of Paris?

_____

m. Why was the Seven Years' War important for Great Britain?

_____

_____

_____

Kärtchen zur Schlacht bei Leuthen (5. Dez. 1757).

17. *Answer the following. (pgs. 61 – 63)*

a. Give **five** reasons why Maria Theresia was a great woman:

- _____
- _____
- _____
- _____
- _____

b. Give **two** ways Maria Theresia preserved and promoted the Catholic Faith in her domains:

- _____
- _____

c. What restrictions did Maria Theresia and Josef II place on the Church in Austria?

_____

_____

_____

d. Give **three** radical reforms Maria Theresia and Josef II made together:

- _____
- _____
- _____

e. What reform did Josef II propose that Maria Theresia would not agree to? _____

_____

f. What action did Maria Theresia reluctantly agree to, causing her to feel guilty the rest of her life?

_____

18. *Match the columns. (pgs. 57 – 63)*

A. Maria Theresia   [   ] fought between France and Great Britain in North America

B. Friedrich II   [   ] first world war in history

C. Franz I   [   ] Polish land seized by Austria

D. Josef II   [   ] the theft of Polish lands by Prussia, Russia, and Austria

E. Katerina the Great   [   ] fought between Austria and Prussia over Silesia

F. West Prussia   [   ] seized Polish lands on the border of Russia

G. French and Indian War   [   ] "true mother of her people"

H. War of Austrian Succession   [   ] Emperor of the Holy Roman Empire; husband of Maria Theresia

I. Seven Years' War   [   ] Polish land seized by Prussia

J. Galicia   [   ] "enlightened despot"

K. First Partition of Poland   [   ] Emperor of the Holy Roman Empire; son of Maria Theresia

19. The map of Europe below shows the Holy Roman (or German) Empire heavily outlined. *Using this map, follow the directions below. (Refer to the maps in Chapter 2 of your textbook as well as an atlas if needed.)*

a. Find these regions and label them: **Austria, Prussia, Bavaria, Saxony, Silesia, Poland, Hungary, Russia, France, Great Britain, Spain**

b. On the countries that were allies of Austria in the Seven Years' War write "A."

c. On the countries that were allies of Prussia in the Seven Years' War write "P."

d. Find the region that Austria lost in the war and put an "X" on it.

e. Find the region taken from Poland by Austria and write "PA" on it.

f. Find the region taken from Poland by Russia and write an "PR" on it.

g. Find the region taken from Poland by Prussia and write "PP" on it. (Hint: This area is the gap between East Prussia and the Prussian kingdom in the Holy Roman Empire.)

Name _____ Date _____

20. *Fill in the blanks. (pgs. 63 – 64)*

> "I have made _____ the legislator of my empire; her _____
> principles shall transform Austria."

After the death of his mother in 1780, Josef II wanted to transform the _____

domains, following the ideas of _____ and _____. However, he did not

want his empire to be a _____ since he wanted to be master and have as much _____ in his

hands as possible. To do this he made many radical changes. He abolished all local _____ throughout his

multicultural empire. He decreed that he himself would make all local _____. He made _____ the

official language of government even in non-_____ speaking regions. He abolished the _____

diet and removed the sacred crown of _____ from Buda to Vienna. His new code of laws allowed

_____ to marry non-_____ and he decreed that marriages no longer required the

_____ of the _____. The _____ alone granted the right to marry and it also permitted

_____. By 1787 Josef had granted his subjects complete _____ freedom which angered the

Austrian bishops. To help the poor, Josef abolished _____ and decreed new _____ for both

peasants and noblemen. He ordered the establishment of Institutes for the _____ to care for the _____

in cities. To compete with Prussia, Josef ordered every _____ in his domains to serve in the _____. This

deeply angered the _____ who did not want their _____ wasting their lives in the endless _____

of Europe. Josef's attempts to take absolute control of all aspects of life began to turn all his people _____ him.

21. *Answer the following. (pgs. 64 – 65)*

a. Give **two** reasons why Josef II initiated reforms in the Church in his domains:

- _____

- _____

b. What name has been given to Josef's radical Church reforms? _____

c. What did Josef forbid bishops to do? _____

d. What was every new bishop required to do? _____

e. Why did Josef despise monks and nuns? _____

_____

f. Because of his attitude toward religious, what did Josef do? _____

_____

_____

_____

_____

g. Give **three** ways Josef tried to regulate the worship and liturgical life of the Church:

- _____
- _____
- _____

h. What were the positive things that Josef did for the Church? _____

_____

_____

i. Why were Josef's reforms a danger to the Church? _____

_____

j. What was the Church's reaction to these reforms? _____

_____

k. Complete Pope Pius VI's prophetic warning to Josef II:

"If you persevere in your projects, _____ of the Faith and the laws of the Church, the hand of the _____ will fall heavily upon you; it will _____ you in the course of your career, it will dig under you an _____ where you will be engulfed in the flower of your _____, and will put an end to the reign that you could have made _____."

l. Give **four** events that turned out badly for Josef II and seemed to fulfill the Pope's prophecy:

- _____
- _____
- _____
- _____

m. What did Josef II do on January 11, 1790? _____

_____

_____

n. Write Josef's mournful epitaph on this tombstone: ➡

✝

B: MARCH 13, 1741
D: FEB. 20, 1790

Did you know? Josef II was buried in the Imperial Crypt, a chamber beneath the Capuchin Church and monastery in Vienna, Austria. The remains of twelve emperors and eighteen empresses are there among the other royal members of the House of Habsburg. Some of the tombs, such as Maria Theresa's, are very ornate; others, such as Josef II's, are plain. The most recent Habsburg entombment in the crypt was in 2011.

Name _____ Date _____

Chapter 3: **The Church Before the Revolution**

1. Write a short biography of St. Paul of the Cross. *(pgs. 69 – 70)*

2. *Answer the following. (pg. 70)*

a. Describe the condition of the Catholic Church in the 18th century. _____

_____

_____

b. What did Voltaire predict about the Church in 1773? _____

_____

c. What was one sign of the demise of Christendom in the 18th century? _____

_____

3. *Match the columns. (pgs. 70 – 71)*

A. Gallicanism   [   ] French word for father

B. papal supremacy   [   ] powerful French family who supported Jansensism

C. papal infallibility [   ] French court of law

D. Gallia   [   ] an abbey of Cistercian nuns and center of the Jansenist movement

E. parlement   [   ] the pope can make no error when teaching on faith and morals

F. Jansenism   [   ] the Latin word for France

G. pere   [   ] the French version of Josephism

H. Port Royal   [   ] joined forces with the Jansenists in calling for a national Church

I. Justinus Febronius   [   ] no person or council can exercise any power over the pope

J. Gallicans   [   ] movement which emphasized austerity and strict penitential practices

K. Arnauld   [   ] pen name of a French bishop who wanted to apply Locke and Rousseau's ideas of government to the Church

4. *Fill in the blank with the correct name. (pgs. 70 – 71)*

a. _____ is the idea the king or secular head of government is in most matters the supreme head of the French Church.

b. _____ decreed that the Church's secular possessions belong to the king of France and that the French supreme court could pass judgement on Church decisions having to do with spiritual matters.

c. _____ decided that he could keep the pope's decrees from being published in France.

d. _____ said that bishops receive their right to rule from the Christian faithful and they are independent of the pope who has no real authority over them.

e. _____ taught that after the Fall, human nature had become so entirely corrupt that, without grace, even our most virtuous acts are sins.

f. _____ thought that most Catholics should receive Communion very infrequently because most Catholics were not capable of perfection contrition.

g. _____ condemned Jansenism

5. *Answer the following. (pg. 72)*

a. Inspired by the Enlightenment and Protestant ideas, what did the foes of the Catholic Church want to do?

_____

_____

b. Give **three** reasons the Church was not prepared to meet the challenges of the 18ᵗʰ century?

- _____
- _____
- _____

6. *Fill in the blanks. (pgs. 72 – 73)*

Out of the _____ popes who reigned between 1700 and 1800, only _____ had the _____ ability, the _____, and the _____ of character to understand the times and to respond ____ to them effectively. One reason inadequate men were made pope was that European _____ had too much influence over the _____ of popes. The men who became popes were the men who the great powers thought would give them no serious _____. Even when a pope did speak against attempts to _____control the Church, the great powers _____ him.

7. Write **five** words or phrases that describe Pope Benedict XIV: *(pg. 74)*

"...but if you want an honest fellow, elect me."

8. *Answer the following. (pgs. 74 & 76)*

a. What did Benedict XIV insist that Catholics had to be to respond the problems of the 18th century?

_____

_____

b. What practice did Benedict XIV begin to communicate to the entire Church?

_____

c. What practical improvements did Benedict XIV make as ruler of the Papal States?

_____

_____

_____

d. Why was Benedict XIV admired even by opponents such as Voltaire?

_____

_____

_____

"If the pope came to London, we should all turn _____."

9. *Circle the correct word or phrase to complete each sentence. (pg. 75)*

a. The Freemasons began as an association of workmen at the time of the **(Medieval/Jewish)** guilds.

b. The Freemasons were a group of **(architects/stonecutters)**.

c. The symbols of the guild were the set square, a trowel, and a workingman's **(pencil/apron)**.

d. Like other guilds, members of the Freemasons, supported one another in their craft and swore to be faithful to the **(Church/liberty of the guild)**.

e. When a great **(earthquake/fire)** destroyed most of London in 1666, the Freemasons helped rebuild the city.

f. Later, the Freemasons became involved in politics when they opposed the **(Tudor/Stuart)** kings in the 17th century.

g. During this time, members of the **(nobility/clergy)** and wealthy merchant class began to join Freemason lodges.

h. By the beginning of the 18th century, the Freemason lodges were no longer gatherings for workingmen, but centers for introducing men to "enlightened" **(work/philosophy)**.

i. Eventually, all the lodges were organized under a Grand Lodge, controlled by members of the **(nobility/Church)**.

j. The traditional symbols of the guild were given new **(mystical/practical)** meanings.

k. Mysterious ceremonies were invented that the members swore to protect with absolute **(secrecy/manpower)**.

l. The new version of Freemasonry **(did not spread/spread)** to other countries from England.

m. It **(was/was not)** clear at first that Freemasonry was anti-Christian or anti-Catholic.

n. Both Voltaire and Benjamin Franklin **(were/were not)** Freemasons.

o. Freemasons believe God is the **(Great Architect/Holy Trinity)** and **(takes care of/ignores)** His creation.

p. Freemasonry **(undermines/helps)** the Catholic Faith and society by encouraging Deism.

q. In 1738, Pope Clement XII **(approved/condemned)** Freemasonry and **(encouraged/forbade)** Catholics to join.

Dig Deeper: Find out more about the Catholic fraternal organization begun by Fr. Michael J. McGivney in the 19th century – the Knights of Columbus. How are the Knights different from the Freemasons?

10. *Complete the following. (pgs. 76 - 77)*

a. Finish this quote from Voltaire:

"Once we have destroyed the _____, we shall have the game in our hands."

b. Give **six** positive accomplishments of the Jesuits:

c. Give **two** just criticisms of the Jesuits:

- _____

- _____

d. What was the main reason the Jesuits were criticized and had enemies?

_____

_____

e. Explain why the Gallicans, Febronians, and Jansenists opposed the **Ultramontane** Jesuits.

_____

_____

_____

f. Describe the Jesuits' Reductions in Paraguay:

_____

_____

_____

_____

_____

_____

11. *Fill in the blanks. (pgs. 77 – 78)*

One of the chief enemies of the Jesuits was Pombal, the "enlightened" _____ of Portugal. His first conflict with the Jesuits was over the Indian _____ the Jesuits had established in _____ America and which Portugal had received from Spain. When the Portuguese government ordered the Indians on the _____ to abandon their lands, many rebelled and Pombal blamed the _____ for the rebellion. Pombal had the royal family's Jesuit _____ dismissed from court. He claimed the Jesuits were behind an _____ attempt on the king. In 1758, Pombal forbade the Jesuits to work in _____. The following year, he seized all Jesuit _____ in Portugal and rounded up all the Jesuits working in Portugal and its _____. Jesuits were exiled, imprisoned and even _____. Pombal also carried on a _____ campaign against the Jesuits, and his lies inspired other _____ to take action against them.

12. *Match the columns. (pgs. 78 – 79 & 81)*

A. Clement XIII   [   ] allowed the Jesuits to continue their work in Silesia

B. Louis XV   [   ] suppressed the Jesuits in the kingdom of Naples

C. Carlos III   [   ] pleasure-loving pope who wanted to restore the Renaissance in Rome

D. Fernando IV   [   ] weak king who made the Jesuits illegal in France

E. Katerina the Great   [   ] weak pope who officially suppressed the Jesuit order in 1773

F. Friedrich the Great   [   ] banished all Jesuits from Spain and its realms overseas

G. Clement XIV   [   ] pope who protested the suppression of the Jesuits in France

H. Pius VI   [   ] allowed the Jesuits to flourish in Russia

13. *Answer the following. (pg. 79)*

a. What reason did Clement XIV give to justify the suppression of the Society of Jesus?

_____

_____

_____

b. Give **two** devastating effects of the suppression of the Society of Jesus:

   • _____

   • _____

c. What do you think Clement XIV meant when he said about the Jesuits, "I have cut off my right hand." ?

_____

_____

_____

_____

_____

14. *Put a check mark in front of the statements that are correct. (pg. 80)*

a. ____ Enlightenment philosophy made more progress among Protestant ministers than among Catholic priests.

b. ____ No Protestants saw the danger the Enlightenment posed for religion.

c. ____ Only Catholics wrote against the dangers of the Enlightenment.

d. ____ Instead of engaging in intellectual battle, some Protestants chose to seek a more personal relationship with God.

e. ____ Pietism is a Catholic movement.

f. ____ Pietists believe pious feelings and becoming more Christlike is more important than dogma.

g. ____ The sense that the world contains mysteries that cannot be grasped by reason is important to pietists.

h. ____ Some Protestants who objected to the Enlightenment also rejected any organized religion.

i. ____ The Society of Friends or Quakers thought the best way to resolve religious differences was through war.

j. ____ The most zealous Christians in the 18th century were the Anglican clergy.

k. ____ Members of the "Holy Club" at Oxford abstained from frivolous amusements, and cultivated religious fervor, piety, and charity.

l. ____ The leader of the Oxford religious group was John Wesley.

m. ____ John Wesley separated from the Anglican Church to form his own religion.

n. ____ Wesleyans or Methodists became one of the largest Protestant denominations in the early United States.

15. *Answer the following. (pgs. 82 – 86)*

a. Give **five** signs of sickness or evil afflicting the Church in the 18th century:

- _____

- _____

- _____

- _____

- _____

b. Complete this statement made by King Louis XVI:

"The _____ of Paris must at least believe in God."

c. Give **four** signs of the Church's health in the 18th century:

- _____
- _____
- _____
- _____

d. Complete this statement made by Rousseau:

> "*I know nothing finer than a _____.*"

e. Give **two** possible reasons why so many turned against the Church at the end of the 18th century:

- _____

  _____

- _____

  _____

f. Why was Spain less affected by the Enlightenment than France and other European countries?

_____

_____

_____

16. *Fill in the name that corresponds to each description: (pgs. 86 – 88)*

a. _____ wrote a rule of life for a new order dedicated to preaching Christ's passion.

b. _____ preached repentance and spread the devotion to the Sacred Heart of Jesus and the Stations of the Cross.

c. _____ gave up a brilliant law career to become a missionary priest and founded the Redemptorists.

Chapter 4: **Revolution in France**

1. *Answer the following. (pgs. 92 – 95)*

a. How did the medieval French government differ from the French government under Louis XVI?

_____

_____

_____

_____

b. What was the chief weakness of the 18th century French government?

_____

_____

c. What were the problems that affected the French nobles?

_____

_____

_____

d. What were the problems that affected the French peasants?

_____

_____

_____

_____

_____

e. Who were the bourgeoisie? _____

_____

_____

f. What kind of reforms did the bourgeoisie want? _____

_____

_____

_____

2. Finish what Count Mirabeau observed: *(pg. 97)*

> *France is ripe for _____."*

3. *Fill in the blanks. (pgs. 95 – 97)*

King Louis XVI was very popular after _____ _____ was defeated in the _____ _____ War. However, soon it became clear that helping the _____ in their war for independence had been ruinously expensive for France. The government was already deep in _____ since it spent far more money than it took in in taxes. Queen _____ and her court frittered away enormous amounts of money on luxuries and pleasures. By 1786, France was near _____ and it seemed nothing could be done to prevent the government's collapse. People throughout France demanded that the King convoke the _____ to solve the country's problems. This representative body had not gathered for _____ years, but faced with growing opposition, the King was forced to issue a decree convening an _____ at Versailles on May 1, 1789.

4. Fill in the blank boxes to complete the political chart of the French government in 1789. *(pg. 100)*

5. *Fill in the blanks. (pgs. 97 – 99)*

The _____ Estate called for the most radical reforms. Not only did they want freedom of the _____ and more just taxes, they wanted _____ for all classes in a united France. However, the _____ Estate would be outnumbered in voting for reforms if the nobles, clergy and commons voted as separate houses. Therefore, the _____ Estate insisted that the first two estates join them in forming one _____. When the king refused to allow this change, the _____ Estate proclaimed itself the _____ _____ of the French people. Prevented from meeting at Versailles, the deputies of the _____ Estate gathered at a nearby _____ court and swore they would not part until they had drawn up a _____ for France. Nobles and _____ joined the revolution. Faced with increasing opposition, the king was forced to given in and recognize the _____ _____ as the legal representative body of the people of France.

"We are here by the will of the _____ and we shall not leave our places except at the point of a _____."

Name _____ Date _____

6. *Match the columns. (pgs. 93 – 101)*

A. bourgeoisie   [   ] armed military force of Paris

B. Marie Antionette   [   ] fortress and prison in Paris

C. Versailles   [   ] wife of King Louis XVI

D. Estates-General   [   ] reform-minded finance minister of France

E. Bastille   [   ] magnificent palace of the French monarchy

F. commune   [   ] the middle class

G. Jacques Necker   [   ] hero of the American Revolution and commander of the National Guard

H. National Guard   [   ] governor of the Bastille; killed by the revolutionaries

I. tricolor cockade   [   ] a body of representatives made up of clergy, nobles, and commoners

J. Lafayette   [   ] replaced the Estates-General as the representative body of France

K. National Assembly   [   ] city government made of elected representatives

L. Launay   [   ] red, blue, and white rosette worn by the French revolutionaries

7. *Answer the following. (pgs. 99 – 102)*

a. What two actions of the king alerted the Parisians that he was planning on crushing the revolution?

_____

_____

b. Why was the Bastille a symbol of absolute monarchy to the Parisians? _____

_____

c. Describe what happened at the Bastille on July 14, 1789: _____

_____

_____

_____

_____

_____

_____

_____

d. How did Louis XVI respond to these events? _____

_____

_____

e. What immediate effects did the revolution have on France? _____

_____

_____

_____

_____

f. What did the National Assembly approve on August 26, 1789? _____

_____

8. Put a check next to the characteristics of the *Declaration of the Rights of Man and of the Citizen. (pgs. 102 – 103)*

a. _____ The king has absolute power.

b. _____ Political authority comes from the people.

c. _____ All Frenchmen are citizens, not subjects.

d. _____ Enlightenment Liberalism became the philosophy of the French state.

e. _____ Law is based on the Eternal Law of God found in the Natural Law.

f. _____ The government's authority comes from God.

g. _____ Law is the general expression of the will of the people.

h. _____ Political authority should be divided among the king, nobles, and commoners.

i. _____ The tax burden should be share equally by all citizens according to their financial ability.

j. _____ The nobility should retain their traditional privileges.

k. _____ Louis XVI was forced to sign the *Declaration* as the only way to keep his throne.

l. _____ The government is the absolute authority over everything and everyone in the state.

m. _____ Every Frenchmen is equal before the law.

n. _____ Every Frenchmen has the right to participate in government.

o. _____ Only Frenchmen who are educated should vote.

p. _____ Men are born free and remain free and equal in rights.

q. _____ It was wholeheartedly supported by Louis XVI.

r. _____ It placed limits on the authority of the king.

9. *Answer the following. (pgs. 102 – 103)*

a. According to the *Declaration*, what are the **four** natural and imprescriptible rights of man?

_____

b. How did the *Declaration* define "liberty"? _____

_____

c. When do citizens have the freedom to exercise their natural rights? _____

_____

d. Who protects the citizens' rights? _____

e. What **two** other rights did the *Declaration* recognize? _____

_____

f. Why <u>didn't</u> the *Declaration* mention the Catholic religion if France was a Catholic country?

_____

10. *Fill in the blanks. (pgs. 104 – 105)*

a. The Assembly granted the king only a _____
veto which gave him little power over laws.

b. The king was not certain how faithful his French _____
were to him, so he had to rely on _____ troops
from _____ to protect him.

c. When the _____ were brought to Versailles,
the Parisians were suspicious and outraged.

d. An armed mob surrounded the palace, forcing the king to surrender to them and return to _____
where he remained a prisoner.

e. The king knew he could not overthrow the _____ alone and he grew fearful for his _____ and
that of his family.

11. *Answer the following. (pgs. 103 – 106)*

a. What problem had the National Assembly failed to address or solve? _____

_____

b. How did Mirabeau suggest this problem be solved? _____

_____

c. What did the Assembly decree on November 2, 1789? _____

_____

d. What religious "reforms" did the Assembly make in February 1790? _____

_____

_____

e. Give **three** changes that the *Civil Constitution of the Clergy* made in France:

- _____
- _____
- _____

f. Give **two** reasons the measures against the Church ended up harming the new revolutionary government:

- _____
- _____

g. Why did Louis XVI sign the *Civil Constitution* even though he was a devout Catholic?

_____

_____

12. *Number the events in the order in which they occurred. (pgs. 106 – 108)*

a. ____ National Assembly called for elections to replace faithful bishops.

b. ____ On April 13, 1791, Pope Pius VI publicly condemned the *Civil Constitution.*

c. ____ In June, the Assembly made it illegal to publish papal decrees in France without government permission.

d. ____ On August 24, 1790, Louis XVI signed the *Civil Constitution.*

e. ____ In May 1791, the National Assembly gave nonjuror priests permission to say Mass again.

f. ____ National Assembly forbade faithful French bishops and priests to preach.

g. ____ French bishops called on the faithful to resist the *Civil Constitution.*

h. ____ November 27, 1790, the Assembly decreed all clergy must take an oath of loyalty to the *Civil Constitution.*

i. _1_ On July 14, 1790, Bishop Talleyrand celebrated the first anniversary of the storming of the Bastille with a Mass.

j. ____ The majority of bishops and priests refuse to take the oath.

k. ____ Nonjuror priests refused to give up their parishes.

l. ____ Full-scale rebellion broke out against the *Civil Constitution* and Constitutional bishops and clergy.

13. In December 1989, the National Assembly redrew the map of France. Explain why it did this and what were the characteristics of the new map. *(pg. 107)*

_____

_____

_____

_____

_____

_____

Name _____ Date _____

14. *Answer the following. (pgs. 108 – 109)*

a. What was Marie Antionette's plan for escape from France? _____

_____

_____

_____

_____

b. What was Mirabeau's alternative plan? _____

_____

_____

_____

_____

c. Why did Mirabeau think his plan was better than the Queen's? _____

_____

_____

d. What plan did Louis XVI choose? Why? _____

_____

_____

e. What was the outcome of the royal family's planned escape? _____

_____

_____

_____

_____

Map to illustrate the FLIGHT to VARENNES

15. *Answer the following. (pg. 110)*

a. Give **four** reforms of the legal system made by the National Assembly:

- _____

- _____

- _____

- _____

b. Whose ideas inspired the Constitution of 1791? _____

_____

c. Explain the Legislative Assembly established by the Constitution of 1791: _____

_____

_____

d. Explain the executive power established by the Constitution of 1791: _____

_____

_____

16. Put a check mark in front of the characteristics of the Constitution of 1791. *(pg. 110)*

a. _____ It was entirely democratic.

b. _____ The lower classes helped design it.

c. _____ The Liberal nobility and bourgeoisie did not trust the common people.

d. _____ It was the first written constitution France had ever had.

e. _____ It gave the king scarcely any power.

f. _____ It only allowed taxpayers and property owners to vote.

g. _____ It granted the suffrage to all citizens.

h. _____ It established a representative government.

i. _____ Citizens voted directly for the candidates of their choice.

j. _____ Citizens voted for electors, who voted for the candidates.

k. _____ Electors always had to vote for the people's choice of candidates.

l. _____ It limited the power of the common man in government and economics.

m. _____ It allowed workers to band together to form unions to protect their rights.

n. _____ It defended the interests of the wealthy bourgeoisie.

o. _____ It was not primarily concerned for the rights of the poor.

Oui

Non

17. *Match the columns. (pgs. 110 – 111)*

A. émigrés   [   ] most extreme of the extremists

B. royalists   [   ] lawyer and extremist member of the National Assembly

C. extremists   [   ] center of the extremist movement

D. Brittany, Anjou, La Vendée   [   ] extremist journal published by Marat

E. Paris   [   ] working class of the cities

F. proletariat   [   ] French nobles who had fled France during the revolution

G. Cordeliers   [   ] wanted to return to the ancient regime and absolute monarchy

H. Jean-Paul Marat   [   ] did not think the revolution had gone far enough

I. *The Friend of the People*   [   ] areas in western France opposed to the new French government

J. Jacobins   [   ] extremist political club

K. Robespierre   [   ] moderate political club that became the most powerful extremist club

18. *Answer the following. (pgs. 111 – 112)*

a. Give **three** changes the extremists wanted to see in the French government:

  • _____

  • _____

  • _____

b. What was the most pressing question facing the National Assembly in the second half of 1791?

  _____

c. What did the moderates think should be done? _____

  _____

d. What did some extremists think should be done? _____

  _____

e. What did Danton suggest? _____

  _____

19. *Fill in the blanks. (pg. 112)*

The _____ presented a petition at the altar on the Champ de Mars, demanding that the king be

tried for _____. Six _____ people signed the petition. The mayor of Paris thought the

gathering was an _____ and declared _____ law. General _____ came to the

Chap de Mars with the National _____ and ordered the crowd to disperse. The crowd defied the order and

the soldiers _____ on them. As the dead fell, the terrified crowd fled. After the _____ at the

Champ de Mars, _____ leaders fled Paris. The government closed several _____ clubs and

banned _____ newspapers. The massacre turned the _____ class more firmly against the

_____.

20. Below is a visual depiction of the divisions in France's new Legislative Assembly. In each bubble, write what characterized that side's political beliefs. *(pgs. 113 – 114)*

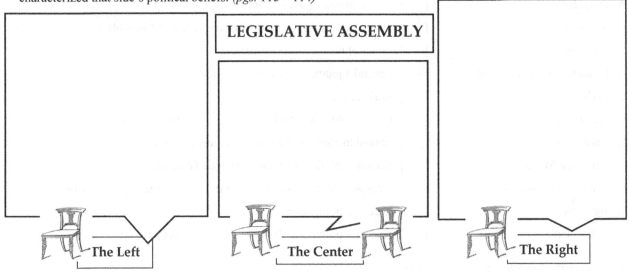

LEGISLATIVE ASSEMBLY

The Left   The Center   The Right

21. *Answer the following. (pg. 114)*

a. Why were the Holy Roman Emperor and the King of Prussia preparing to wage war against France?

_____

_____

b. Even though France was not prepared for war, why did Louis XVI want war?

_____

_____

c. Why did the Feuillants want war? _____

_____

d. Why did the Girondins want war? _____

_____

e. Why did Robespierre and Marat oppose the war? _____

_____

22. *Circle the correct word or phrase in **bold** to complete the sentence. (pg. 115)*

a. **(Leopold II/Franz II)** accused France of acts of injustice against the **(pope/king)** and certain imperial princes.

b. The National Assembly demanded that Franz remove his troops on the **(Hungarian/French)** border and expel the French **(émigrés/extremists)** from his territories.

c. When Franz ignored these demands, **(Louis XVI/National Assembly)** declared war on him on April 20, 1792.

d. **(Lafayette/Duke of Brunswick)** was made the supreme commander of the French army.

e. The French people were filled with **(dread/enthusiasm)** for the war and **(eagerly/reluctantly)** volunteered to fight the enemies of the revolution.

f. Since the French army was **(the best in Europe/poorly trained and undisciplined)**, their first battles against the allied armies of Austria and Prussia were **(humiliating defeats/glorious victories)**.

g. **(Robespierre/Louis XVI)** was in secret contact with the enemy and Marie Antionette was supplying them with **(arms/battle plans)**.

h. The people of Paris stormed the palace, demanding the **(death/overthrow)** of the king.

23. *Answer the following. (pg. 115)*

a. What were the **five** goals of the allied forces according to the Duke of Brunswick's manifesto?

■ _____

■ _____

■ _____

■ _____

■ _____

b. What would the allied forces do if the French did not lay down their arms? _____

_____

_____

c. The manifesto convinced the extremists in Paris of what? _____

_____

24. *Match the columns. (pgs. 115 – 116)*

A. August 3, 1792   [   ]royal palace in Paris

B. August 9, 1792   [   ]group in charge of writing up a new
                                  constitution for France

C. August 10, 1792   [   ]new government established to replace
                                  the monarchy

D. Tuileries   [   ]Paris extremists demand that the king
                                  be deposed.

E. Tower of the Temple   [   ]group of six ministers that replaced the
                                  king as the executive power

F. National Convention   [   ] Revolutionary commune seizes control
                                  of Paris's city government.

G. Executive Council   [   ]medieval fortress where they royal family was imprisoned

H. republic   [   ]Parisians attack the Tuileries and the Legislative Assembly deposes and
                                  imprisons the king

25. *Answer the following. (pgs. 116 – 118)*

a. Describe the conditions in France after the overthrow of the king. _____
_____
_____
_____

b. Who was the new leader of the French government? _____

c. What were the September Massacres? _____
_____
_____
_____

d. Who commanded the French army as the allied forces marched toward Paris?
_____

e. Describe what happened at Valmy on September 20, 1792: _____
_____
_____
_____

f. Why were the allies willing to negotiate with Danton's deputies? _____
_____
_____

g. What was the outcome of the negotiations? _____
_____

h. Why were Frenchmen filled with new confidence after Valmy? _____
_____

i. What did many Frenchmen hope to do? _____
_____

j. Finish the German poet Goethe's prophecy after the battle of Valmy:

"On this day begins _____
_____."

LIBERTÉ,
ÉGALITÉ,
FRATERNITÉ
OU LA MORT

Chapter 5: Many Revolutions

1. *Answer the following. (pgs. 123 - 125)*

a. Why did Danton fail to unify the new government of France? _____

_____

_____

b. What political party did Danton belong to? _____

c. What ideal did the Left and the Right in the French government agree on? _____

_____

d. What did Danton think the boundaries of France should be? _____

_____

e. Why did Danton think France needed a strong central government? _____

_____

f. Who was France fighting at this time? _____

_____

g. Why did Danton want to keep peace with Great Britain? _____

_____

h. Why did the Girondins oppose a strong central government? _____

_____

2. *Below is a visual depiction of the divisions in France's National Convention. In each bubble, write the political beliefs of each side. (pgs. 123 – 124)*

NATIONAL CONVENTION

The Left
(Jacobins & Cordeliers)

The Center or Plain

The Right
(Girondins)

3. *Answer the following. (pg. 125)*

a. Why did the Jacobins fear Louis XVI? _____

_____

b. What was the chief charge against Louis XVI? _____

_____

c. What was the evidence against Louis XVI? _____

_____

d. Why objections did the Girondins have against putting the king on trial? _____

_____

_____

e. What motivated the Jacobins and many of the French to put the king on trial?

_____

4. *Number the events in the order in which they occurred. (pgs. 125 – 126)*

a. ___ Louis XVI makes his will.

b. ___ The deputies of the National Convention vote on the king's punishment.

c. ___ The Convention declares Louis XVI will be executed by guillotine on January 21, 1793.

d. ___ The Girondins make their final appeal to save the king.

e. ___ An indictment of the king is presented to the Convention.

f. ___ The votes are tallied with the majority voting for death.

g. ___ The Convention decides the king is guilty of treason.

h. ___ Louis and his lawyers appear before the Convention to present their defense.

i. ___ The deputies debate for two weeks.

j. _1_ The Jacobins present their allegations of the king's treason to the Convention deputies.

5. *Finish Louis XVI's last words: (pgs. 126 – 127)*

"I die _____
_____
_____
_____
_____
_____."

6. *What did the crowd shout when they saw the king's severed head?*

Name _____ Date _____

7. *Answer the following. (pgs. 129 – 131)*

a. Give **three** reasons why the English turned against the French:

- _____

- _____

- _____

b. Why did France declare war on Great Britain? _____

_____

c. What event destroyed the absolute monarchy in England? _____

_____

d. What governing body became the chief power in England instead of the king? _____

e. Name **three** things the king of England could no longer do according to the 1689 Declaration of Rights signed by King William III.

- _____

- _____

- _____

8. *Follow the directions below. (pg. 132)*

a. On the map on the right, find and label:

France   England   Scotland   Wales   Ireland

English Channel   Atlantic Ocean   North Sea

b. Put an **X** on the countries that the British king ruled in the 18th century.

c. Circle the body of water English soldiers would need to cross to get to France.

Extra: Below is the flag of Great Britain. Find out what its colors are and fill it in.

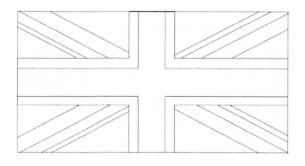

9. *The phrases below describe the two parties in the British Parliament. If the phrase describes the Whig party, write "W" on the line. If the phrase describes the Tory party, write "T" on the line. If it describes both parties, write "WT" on the line. (pgs. 131 & 134)*

a. _____ supported the Church of England (Anglicans)

b. _____ wanted the king to have a very limited role in government

c. _____ supported the traditional role of the king, but not absolute monarchy

d. _____ some wanted to restore the House of Stuart to the throne

e. _____ represented the class of people engaged in commerce

f. _____ objected to the office of prime minister

g. _____ conservatives

h. _____ wanted no radical changes in government or English society

i. _____ believed the rich and wellborn should govern because of their superior wisdom and abilities

j. _____ supported the radical Protestant groups

k. _____ became the chief party under King George I and King George II

l. _____ loved pompous royal ceremonies

m. _____ party name comes from a slang word for an Irish Catholic outlaw

n. _____ wanted Parliament to have much more power than the king

o. _____ supported measures that kept the oligarchy in power

p. _____ represented the people of England, Scotland and Wales

10. *Fill in the blanks. (pgs. 132 – 133)*

The British Constitution is not a _____ document. Unlike the French or U.S. Constitution, no committee came together to design it all at one time. Rather, it is a set of _____ and governmental procedures that have arisen over _____ simply from the practice of governing. Some _____ laws such as the _____ Carta and the Declaration of Rights form part of the British Constitution. The head of the British government was the king whose powers were limited by a _____. This form of government is called a _____ monarchy. Although all laws were made in the king's name, _____ made laws, not the king. The king had the power only to _____ laws. Neither could the king levy _____. Even though he was the _____ _____ of the armed forces, he could not maintain an army without funds from _____. He also relied on _____ for an allowance for his own personal support.

Name _____   Date _____

11. *Answer the following. (pgs. 133 – 134)*

a. Who could had the right to vote in the rural districts of Great Britain? _____

_____

b. Who was not able to vote in the rural districts? _____

_____

c. How could local aristocrats control elections in rural districts? _____

_____

d. How did the local aristocrats know who people voted for? _____

_____

e. Which towns (or boroughs) had the right to send representatives to Parliament? _____

_____

f. Who controlled the elections in these towns? _____

_____

g. How were "rotten boroughs" able to send representatives to Parliament? _____

_____

h. What kind of men controlled Parliament by the late 18th century? _____

_____

12. *Match the columns. (pgs. 129 – 134)*

A. regicide   [   ] representatives of the rural population

B. Whig   [   ] upper house of Parliament

C. Tory   [   ] government by a few for their own benefit

D. prime minister   [   ] representatives of the towns

E. constitutional monarchy   [   ] lower house of Parliament

F. House of Lords   [   ] killing or assassination of a king

G. House of Commons   [   ] head of Parliament

H. Lords Spiritual   [   ] conservative party in the British government

I. Lords Temporal   [   ] bishops of the Church of England

J. Knights of the Shire   [   ] hereditary or recently ennobled aristocrats

K. burgesses   [   ] radical party in the British government

L. oligarchy   [   ] government with a king whose powers are limited by a constitution

13. *Answer the following. (pgs. 134 – 135)*

a. Give **four** sources of Great Britain's wealth in the 18th century:

- _____
- _____
- _____
- _____

b. What did members of the British nobility and wealthy middle class do with their wealth to become wealthier?

_____

c. What economic system became predominant in Great Britain in the 18th century? _____

d. Define this system: _____

_____

_____

_____

e. What traditional economic system did it replace? _____

14. Put a check mark in front of the characteristics of the capitalist system. *(pgs. 135 – 137)*

a. _____ controlled by regulations that discouraged competition

b. _____ organized into trades

c. _____ large-scale organization

d. _____ allows more people to own businesses

e. _____ workers control only their labor

f. _____ workers sell their labor for a wage

g. _____ shares new inventions with other businesses

h. _____ relies on loans from banks

i. _____ provides for the spiritual and material needs of workers

j. _____ small-scale, family-centered

k. _____ not controlled by any regulations

l. _____ impersonal

m. _____ chief economic system of Europe until the 17th century

n. _____ few own and control wealth producing enterprises

o. _____ prohibits businesses from trying to drive one another out of business

p. _____ many laborers are hired by those with wealth to engage in activities that increase wealth

Name _____ Date _____

15. *Answer the following. (pgs. 136 – 138)*

a. Name **three** 18th century scientific discoveries that set the stage for the Industrial Revolution.

   _____   _____   _____

b. What **two** inventions caused dramatic changes in the textile industry? _____

   _____

c. How did James Watt's invention changed where factories were built? _____

   _____

d. Why did banks become more important and influential in British society because of the Industrial Revolution?

   _____

   _____

e. Describe the working and living conditions of British factory workers.

   _____

   _____

   _____

   _____

   _____

f. What did many workers do to protest the factory system? _____

   _____

   _____

g. In response to the struggle between workers and employers, what did Parliament make illegal in 1799?

   _____

h. Why did Parliament side with employers? _____

   _____

16. *Fill in the blanks. (pg. 137)*

The capitalist justification of the treatment of workers was based on the Enlightenment economic theory called

_____. This French word embodies the idea that economic activity should be completely

_____ and not bound by any _____. This doctrine was further developed by Adam Smith in his

work, "_____." Smith said that _____ should not try to

control economic activity by regulating _____ or _____ or by any _____

whatsoever. Each person should be allowed to follow his own personal _____ in the creation of

_____ for himself. Smith believed that economic activity was led by an "_____ hand" or

natural laws that would lead society to prosperity.

17. *Match the columns. (pgs. 138 – 139)*

A. commons   [   ] small farmer who cultivates his own land

B. open fields   [   ] taxes to support the poor

C. strip field farming   [   ] area adjoining farmland where peasants pastured their farm animals

D. subsistence farming   [   ] farmers received strips of common land for personal cultivation

E. yeoman   [   ] place to care for the poor at public expense

F. enclosed field farming   [   ] arable land held in common by a farming village

G. market farming   [   ] produces for the farm family's needs first, then sells any extra

H. workhouse   [   ] divided the common land into fenced off, compact farmsteads

I. poor-rates   [   ] produces primarily to sell

18. *Answer the following. (pgs. 138 – 141)*

a. Explain how land had traditionally been divided for farming until the 18th century.

_____

_____

_____

b. Give **four** developments in the methods of farming that made it more "scientific" in the 18th century:

- _____
- _____
- _____
- _____

c. What benefit did these methods have? _____

_____

d. What did landholders do in order to use the new methods of farming? _____

_____

_____

e. What was different about the enclosures in the 18th century from previous enclosures?

_____

f. Who benefitted mostly from the enclosures? _____

g. Who suffered the most from the enclosures? _____

h. Explain the effect the enclosure of lands had on peasant farmers: _____

_____

_____

_____

_____

i. What effect did the enclosures have on the countryside of England and Wales? _____

_____

_____

j. Why did the enclosures make it much harder for the poor to better their condition?

_____

_____

_____

k. What effect did the enclosures have on the morality of the rural poor? _____

_____

_____

Did you know? Workhouses were often harsh and degrading places. They were charitable institutions, yet many English believed the poor should be punished and treated harshly to "reform" them. Besides the destitute poor, orphans with no one to care for them also ended up there. In Charles Dicken's novel *Oliver Twist,* the main character, Oliver, grows up in a workhouse. There is a famous scene from the book wherein a still hungry Oliver begs for more gruel. "Please, sir, I want some more." Oliver is cruelly punished for his request. Many of Dicken's novels paint a vivid picture of the life of the poor in England's cities after the Industrial Revolution.

19. *Write the name of the person who fits each description. (pgs. 141 – 142)*

a. _____ was a German prince and king of Great Britain. He had a strong sense his kingship and challenged Parliament by appointing Tory ministers when Whigs were in the majority.

b. _____ was the popular Tory prime minister and defender of the king against his enemies in Parliament. He initially called for government reforms, but gave up after his reform bill was defeated

c. _____ was a Whig statesman and one of the king's opponents. Although he had a bad moral reputation, he had genuine concern for the poor and oppressed and urged government reforms. He admired the French Revolution.

d. _____ was a Whig statesman who detested and condemned the French Revolution and demanded war against France.

20. *Answer the following. (pgs. 142 – 143)*

a. Give the **five** reforms Charles Fox pushed for:

- _____
- _____
- _____
- _____
- _____

b. According to Edmund Burke, what was the source of any rights humans have? _____

_____

_____

c. Why did Burke think it was necessary to put down revolution? _____

_____

_____

d. Why did British government reforms never happen even though there was much talk about reform?

_____

_____

e. Why did Pitt threaten to punish anyone who spoke out in favor of reforms?

_____

_____

f. What turned the English against the French Revolution even more than the threat of punishment?

_____

_____

_____

Chapter 6: The Rise and Fall of Jacobin France

1. *Answer the following. (pgs. 147 – 149)*

a. Give **three** reasons the working class of Paris was suffering and easily pushed to violence.

- _____
- _____
- _____

b. Why did the working class of Paris and other extremists hate the Girondins?

_____

_____

c. Why did Danton think the government needed greater power? _____

_____

d. What was the Committee of Public Safety? What powers did it have? _____

_____

_____

_____

2. *Circle the correct word or phrase in bold to complete the sentence. (pgs. 147 – 149)*

a. France needed many more troops to fight its growing list of enemies, so the Convention demanded 300,000 men by **(conscription/volunteer)**.

b. The fanatic **(Girondins/Jacobins)** had grown very strong and wanted to force the **(Girondins/Jacobins)** out of the Convention.

c. The **(sans-culottes/laissez-faire)** were the poor working class of Paris and they were on the brink of riot.

d. Extremists like the **(Girondins/Enragés)** could easily provoke a revolt in Paris.

e. Food and necessities were being hoarded by the **(merchants/nobility)** and being sold at high prices for large profit.

f. The **(king/Liberals)** had removed regulations on business and defended the **(enragés/laissez-faire)** principle that allowed one to sell goods at whatever price one wished.

g. To control France more firmly, the Convention established the **(Revolutionary Tribunal/Central Bureaucracy of Dictators)** that had the authority to try and convict anyone suspected of conspiring against the revolution.

h. General **(Danton/Dumouriez)** turned against the revolutionary government and tried to convince the army to overthrow the Convention and restore the **(monarch/republic)**.

i. In the end, the revolutionary government had **(more/less)** absolute power than the king had possessed and went against its ideal of **(the common good/individual freedom)**.

3. *Fill in the blanks. (pgs. 149 – 151)*

The Catholic Faith remained the center of life in the _____ region of France in spite of the revolution. Peasants there were discontent because of the revolutionary government's attacks on their _____ and they revolted when the Convention tried to force the peasants to _____ for the government. The peasants formed an army under the leadership of a fellow peasant and pious man named _____ _____. They called themselves the _____ and _____ Army. They wanted to restore the _____ to France, but they primarily fought for their _____. Their insignia was the _____ of Jesus surmounted by a _____. The peasants were fierce and recklessly charged the enemy even though they were poorly _____. By the end of May 1793, this ragtag army had defeated the _____ troops in several battles and had captured the chief city of the _____.

4. *Below are the steps that led to the Jacobins gaining control of the government of France. Fill in the missing words. (pgs. 151 – 153)*

1. On April 2, 1793, _____ pleads unsuccessfully for the peace between the Girondins and Jacobins.

2. The Jacobin Club and the Paris sections demand that the Convention indict the _____ leaders as enemies of the revolution.

3. The Girondins demand that the Convention indict _____ for plotting violence against the government.

4. The Paris sections present a petition demanding that the Convention dismiss 22 _____ leaders as "guilty of felony to the sovereign people."

5. Intimidated by the mob, the Convention tries and acquits _____ on April 24, 1793.

6. On May 3, 1793, the _____ oppose a measure to place a maximum price on grain.

7. On May 18, a _____ deputy demands that the Convention dissolve the Paris commune.

8. The Convention forms a _____ to investigate conspiracy against the government.

9. The Convention arrests two _____ leaders and Jacques _____.

10. On May 25, the Paris _____ denounces the arrests and demands the release of _____.

11. In a fiery speech, the _____ leader, Maximilien _____ threatens the destruction of Paris.

12. _____ calls for the people to rise in revolt against the corrupt deputies.

13. The National Convention releases _____ but refuses to disband the _____.

14. On May 31, the _____ sound the tocsin for revolt.

15. The Convention agrees to abolish the _____.

16. Danton advises the _____ leaders to voluntarily resign to restore peace.

17. The deputies leave the _____ and seek protection from the National Guard.

18. Armed men stop the deputies and threaten to shoot them if they do not return to the _____.

19. The deputies are forced to vote on the indictment of the _____.

20. On June 2, 1793, thirty-one _____ are condemned and made prisoners of the Convention.

21. The power of the _____ is broken and the _____ are triumphant.

5. *Answer the following (pgs. 154 – 155)*

a. Give **two** ways the Constitution of 1793 was different than the Constitution of 1791.

- _____

- _____

b. Why did Constitution of 1793 never go into effect? _____

_____

c. What were the **two** main dangers facing France?

- _____

- _____

d. What did Danton ask the Convention to do in order to respond to these dangers?

_____

_____

e. What measure did the Convention vote in on August 23, 1793? _____

_____

f. What additional requirements did the measure demand? _____

_____

_____

_____

6. *Match the columns. (pgs. 153 – 156)*

A. Robespierre   [   ] radical and bloodthirsty leader of the *Enragés*

B. Antoine de Saint-Just   [   ] French port city, given over to Great Britain by loyalists

C. Charlotte Corday   [   ] in charge of building up and organizing the revolutionary armed forces

D. Jacques Hébert   [   ] powerful leader of the Jacobins

E. Lazare Carnot   [   ] act allowing the arrest of anyone suspected of being a counterrevolutionary

F. Louis XVII   [   ] zealous and fanatic follower of Rousseau's philosophy

G. Napoleone Buonaparte   [   ] poor nobleman's daughter who murdered Marat in revenge

H. Toulon   [   ] period of great bloodshed to purge France of the enemies of the revolution

I. Law of Suspects   [   ] son of Marie Antoinette and Louis XVI; heir to the French throne

J. Reign of Terror   [   ] young Corsican army officer whose plan enabled the revolutionaries to
                                  regain Toulon

7. *Answer the following. (pgs. 156 – 158)*

a. What was the fate of Marie Antoinette? _____

_____

_____

b. Describe what happened to Lyons and its citizens. _____

_____

_____

_____

c. Describe what happened in Toulon after it fell to the revolutionary army. _____

_____

d. How did Jean-Baptiste Carrier kill his prisoners? _____

_____

e. Describe what happened in the Vendée after the Vendeans were defeated. _____

_____

_____

_____

8. *Fill in the blanks. (pgs. 159 – 160)*

Many revolutionaries were not satisfied with a state Church, they wanted to _____ the Church altogether and replace it with worship of the _____. The revolutionary government took over functions that had been performed by the Church: providing for the _____ and _____; overseeing the foundation of _____ and their _____; registering _____ and _____. Finally, the state made itself master of the family by permitting _____. The Convention ordered nonjuror priests to be _____ or _____ to French colonies. Even Constitutional bishops objected when the Convention ordered them to permit priests to _____. Some Constitutional priests refused to _____ the marriage of couples who were unbaptized or _____. In July and October of 1793, the Convention passed laws to _____ Constitutional bishops or priests who refused to violate the Church teaching on _____. In November, the Constitutional archbishop of Paris and several of his clergy renounced their _____ before the Convention and called for the worship of _____ and _____ instead of God. The cathedral of Notre Dame in Paris was turned into a _____ of _____ and a shrine to the _____ of _____ was placed in the sanctuary. A popular _____, Mademoiselle Maillard, was carried through the streets of Paris to Notre Dame and was enthroned as the _____ of _____ in a grotesque ceremony. Soon all the _____ in Paris were seized and Catholic _____ in them was forbidden. The Mass was replaced by _____ of _____. This new religion of the republic spread throughout France.

9. Give **four** facts about the Revolutionary Calendar: *(pg. 159)*

- _____
  _____

- _____
  _____

- _____
  _____

- _____
  _____

10. *Answer the following. (pgs. 161 – 163)*

a. Why did Danton oppose the Law of Suspects and the Terror? _____
   _____
   _____

b. What were the **three** forces in Paris that supported the Terror? _____
   _____

c. What did Danton think he needed to do to end the Terror? _____
   _____

d. What were Robespierre's beliefs about religion? _____
   _____
   _____

e. What did Robespierre do when he was forced to choose between his allies on the Committee and Danton?
   _____

f. How did Carnot's victories on the battlefield help Danton's cause? _____
   _____

g. Why was Robespierre not willing to end the Terror? _____
   _____
   _____

h. What was the fate of Danton? _____

i. Finish Danton's ominous prediction:

   "Robespierre, _____."

11. *Fill in the blanks. (pgs. 164 – 166)*

a. The Committee, the Convention, and even the Jacobins feared Robespierre because he was tremendously
_____ and had become the _____ of France.

b. Deputies said of Robespierre, "He is not satisfied with being master, he must be _____."

c. The people of Paris began to turn against Robespierre because the Terror was growing _____ and some
_____ victims had been executed.

d. To establish his power more firmly, Robespierre had all the revolutionary _____ placed under the
control of the Committee of _____ and he replaced the elected _____ of
Paris with a member of the Committee.

e. To further the establishment of a civic religion for France, Robespierre proposed the Festival of the _____
_____. This Deist form of worship was held on June 8, _____. The procession in the streets of Paris to
the Champ de Mars was led by _____.

f. Two days after the festival, Robespierre presented a law that vastly expanded the power of the Revolutionary
_____ and allowed it to condemn people of _____ without any _____.

g. With the passage of this law, the Terror entered its _____ phase. In six weeks, _____ victims
were guillotined.

h. During those six weeks, the _____ nuns of Compiégne were condemned as "enemies of the
people" and executed.

12. *Answer the following. (pgs. 166 – 167)*

a. How did the Convention first declare its opposition to Robespierre?

_____

_____

_____

b. While defending himself, what did Robespierre call on the Convention to do?

_____

_____

c. How did Barére foil Robespierre's attempt to bring the Convention to his side? _____

_____

_____

d. Why did Robespierre refuse to stir up a revolt against the Convention? _____

_____

e. What did the deputies cry out after Saint-Just accused several members of the Convention of treason?

_____

f. What was the fate of Robespierre? _____

_____

13. *Answer the following. (pgs. 167 – 171)*

a. Give **four** changes the Convention made after the fall of Robespierre:

- _____
- _____
- _____
- _____

b. What change did the Convention make that hurt the working class? _____

_____

c. Give **four** benefits given to the Vendeans by the Convention.

- _____
- _____
- _____
- _____

d. Why was there great suffering in Paris during the winter of 1794 – 1795? _____

_____

_____

e. What did this misery and the harangues of the Jacobins inspire the working class to do?

_____

f. What did the Convention do in response? _____

_____

_____

g. What did the sans-culottes demand of the Convention? _____

_____

h. What two events worked against the plans of the monarchists and royalist to restore the monarchy?

_____

_____

i. Instead of reviving the democratic Constitution of 1793 or restoring the monarchy, what did the Convention do?

_____

j. Describe the legislative branch under the Constitution of Year III. _____

_____

_____

k. Describe the executive branch under the Constitution of Year III. _____

_____

l. What was the new government under the Constitution of Year III called? _____

m. How did the Convention keep monarchists or royalists from being elected to the new government?

_____

n. How did Parisians and royalists respond to this? _____

_____

o. Explain Napoleon Bonaparte's role in saving the Convention and the revolution. _____

_____

_____

_____

_____

_____

14. *Match the columns. (pgs. 167 – 171)*

A. Thermidorians   [   ] those who wanted to restore the ancient monarchy

B. Insurrection of 12th Germinal   [   ] constitution that was neither monarchical nor fully democratic

C. Insurrection of the 1st Prairial   [   ] new government established by the Constitution of Year III

D. constitutional monarchists   [   ] lower house of the National Assembly; members were at least 30 years old

E. royalists   [   ] revolt of working people and poor on May 20, 1795

F. legitimists   [   ] executive authority; 5 members chosen by the National Assembly

G. Louis Stanislaus   [   ] upper house of the National Assembly; members were at least 40 years old

H. Constitution of 1793   [   ] those who want a king with power limited by a constitution

I. Constitution of Year III   [   ] deputies who brought about Robespierre's fall; leaders of the Convention

J. Council of 500   [   ] brilliant military mind who defended the Convention against the insurgents

K. Council of Ancients   [   ] democratic constitutional approved, but never enacted

L. Directors   [   ] brother of Louis XVI; heir to the throne after the death of Louis XVII

M. Directory   [   ] revolt of working people and poor on April 1, 1795

N. Two-Thirds Law   [   ] supporters of a traditional kingly line

O. Napoleone Buonaparte   [   ] decreed only one-third of the legislature could be new members; the
                                               remaining members had to be chosen from existing Convention members

Chapter 7: The Triumph of the "Little Corporal"

1. Write a fact about Napoleon Bonaparte's early life in each box. *(pg. 178)*

2. *Answer the following. (pgs. 177 – 182)*

a. Why did the French invade Italy? _____

_____

_____

b. How did Napoleon become the hero of France and the French Republic? _____

_____

_____

c. What did Napoleon think about the Catholic Faith and the Church? _____

_____

_____

d. What did the French government want Napoleon to do in Rome? _____

_____

e. Did Napoleon obey the Directory? _____

f. What did Napoleon demand of Pius VI in the armistice at Bologna? _____

_____

g. What was the outcome of Napoleon's nine-month battle against the Austrians?

_____

_____

h. What did Pius VI have to give up in the Treaty of Tolentino? _____

_____

3. *Fill in the blanks. (pgs. 183 – 184)*

a. In the French legislative election of 1797, the majority of seats went to candidates who favored a constitutional

_____ and wanted to reconcile the new government with the _____.

b. On September 4, 1797, the radicals staged a _____, seized power, and purged the government of non-radicals.

c. The newly purged French government enacted measures against _____ and the _____.

d. In February 1798, the French marched against Rome and took Pope Pius VI _____.

e. General Berthier proclaimed Rome a _____ and Pius VI was

_____ from the city.

f. The elderly and ill Pius died a year and a half later in _____.

g.

> "May my successor, whoever he may be, _____ the French as sincerely as I do."

4. *Number the events in the order they occurred. (pgs. 185 – 189)*

a. ____ Napoleon's Army of the Orient successfully conquers Egypt.

b. ____ Arriving in Paris, Napoleon plots with Sieyés and others to overthrow the French government.

c. ____ Napoleon returns to Paris a hero and each political faction tries to win him to its side.

d. ____ The British navy under Admiral Horatio Nelson destroys the French fleet at the mouth of the Nile.

e. ____ Napoleon retreats to Egypt, and leaving his troops there, secretly returns to France on August 23, 1799.

f. _1_ Napoleon concludes a permanent peace treaty with Austria.

g. ____ Napoleon tries unsuccessfully to conquer Palestine and Syria.

h. ____ Napoleon sets out to conquer Egypt in order to cut off Great Britain's communications with India.

i. ____ Three men are appointed consuls to govern France, with Napoleon as first consul (or dictator).

j. ____ On November 10, 1799, Napoleon leads troops to the National Assembly and forces the delegates to flee.

k. ____ In the fall of 1799, Emmanuel-Joseph Sieyés comes up with a plan to replace the Directory.

l. ___ While Napoleon is in Egypt, the Directory loses everything the French had gained in Europe. and many fear the Directory is leading France into ruin.

5. Complete the sequence of change in France's government over 10 years: *(pg. 189)*

Absolute _____

constitutional _____

_____

_____

6. *Circle the correct word or phrase in* **bold** *to complete each sentence. (pgs. 189 - 191)*

a. On November 30, 1799, cardinals gathered in **(Venice/Rome)** to elect a new pope.

b. Because the conclave was **(scared of Napoleon/split by factions)**, it took the cardinals four months to agree on a papal candidate.

c. On March 14, 1800, they finally elected Barnaba Chiaramonti, an Italian bishop and a **(Jesuit/Benedictine)**.

d. Besides being very devout, kind, firm, and generous with the poor, Chiaramonti believed democracy **(was/was not)** opposed to the Gospel of Christ.

e. Even though Chiaramonti **(did not/did)** love the French republic, he was willing to make **(peace/war)** with it.

f. Chiaramonti thought preserving the pope's spiritual authority was **(far more important than/ just as important as)** salvaging his temporal power as lord of the Papal States.

g. Chiaramonti's coronation as Pope Pius VII took place in **(St. Peter's Basilica/the monastery of San Giorgio)**.

h. When Pius VII finally returned to Rome, he began **(repairing the damage done by/gathering an army to fight)** the revolution.

i. The pope passed edicts to restore public **(executions/morality)** and he **(punished/pardoned)** his enemies.

7. *Match the columns. (pgs. 191 – 193)*

A. Vendeans [ ] French victory against the Austrians near Munich

B. Army of the Rhine [ ] brought peace between Austria and France

C. Army of the Reserve [ ] region of northern Italy captured by Napoleon

D. St. Bernard [ ] laid down their arms after Napoleon promised them complete freedom of religion

E. Fort Bard [ ] its navy remained at war with France

F. Genoa [ ] great victory for Napoleon in which he defeated the Austrians despite being outnumbered and outgunned

G. Battle of Marengo [ ] perilous pass in the Alps which Napoleon crossed to invade Italy

H. Lombardy [ ] small castle that guarded the pass into the Lombard plain

I. Battle of Hohenlinden [ ] French force that fought the allies in Germany

J. Treaty of Luneville [ ] surrendered to the Austrians after a bitter siege

K. Great Britain [ ] French force led by Napoleon into Italy

8. What did Napoleon win for himself with the Battle of Marengo? *(pg. 192)*

_____

_____

_____

9. *Answer the following. (pgs. 193 – 196)*

a. How did Napoleon solve France's bankruptcy crisis? _____
_____
_____

b. What reform of Napoleon's had the most long-lasting effect? _____
_____

c. Give **three** ways Napoleon tried to make France more self-sufficient:

- _____

- _____

- _____

d. Give **three** public works that Napoleon initiated:

- _____

- _____

- _____

e. Why did Napoleon want the émigrés or French exiles to come back to France? _____
_____

f. How did he get the émigrés to return to France? _____
_____
_____

g. What had helped lead to the downfall of the Directory? _____
_____

h. What did Napoleon want to do so the same thing would not happen to his government?
_____
_____

i. What ended the schism between the Constitutional Church of France and Rome?
_____

j. Why was Pope Pius VII not entirely happy with the concordat? _____
_____
_____

k. Overall, how did Napoleon treat the Catholic Church? _____
_____
_____

Name _____   Date _____

10. *Fill in the blanks. (pgs. 196 – 197)*

On Christmas Eve in 1800, somebody tried to _____ Napoleon. This attempt convinced

Napoleon that he needed to strengthen the _____ police. Police _____ on government

enemies intensified and the _____ service opened _____ to detect plots against the government.

Napoleon established strict _____ over the newspapers and the theatre. Napoleon feared that when

his term as First Consul was over, his enemies would _____ his reforms. To keep this from happening,

he wanted to be made First Consul for _____. The senators did not want Napoleon to have so much _____

and voted only to extend his term for another _____ years. However, when a plebiscite was called, a large majority

of the French people _____ to make Napoleon First Consul for _____. On August 4, 1802, the Senate

confirmed Napoleon as First Consul for _____ and gave him the right to name his _____.

Napoleon did not have the title of _____, but he had the powers of a _____.

11. *True or false? (pgs. 197 – 198)*

a. _____ King George III allowed the Bourbon princes to live in England and even supported them with money.

b. _____ The English newspapers ridiculed Napoleon.

c. _____ Admiral Horatio Nelson admired and respected Napoleon.

d. _____ Napoleon had gained more land for France.

e. _____ England was happy France had gained more power in Europe.

f. _____ Napoleon planned to invade England.

g. _____ England tried to make peace with Napoleon.

h. _____ Napoleon sold the Louisiana Territory to the U.S. because he needed money.

i. _____ France declared war on Great Britain on May 16, 1803.

j. _____ The French Bourbon princes plotted to have Napoleon assassinated.

k. _____ The Duke of Enghien, a relative of the Bourbons, was involved in the conspiracy against Napoleon.

l. _____ Enghien was arrested and after a fair trial, was acquitted.

m. _____ His treatment of Enghien showed that Napoleon was a great defender of freedom and justice.

12. *Fill in the blanks. (pgs. 199 –202)*

a. Many in France thought kingship was anti_____.

b. On May 18, 1804, when the Senate unanimously offered Napoleon the _____, they gave him the title _____ Napoleon I, ruler of the French _____.

c. Napoleon saw himself as the new _____.

d. To make his new title legitimate, Napoleon decided he needed to be _____ by the pope.

e. Napoleon commanded Pius VII to come to _____ to perform the ceremony.

f. Pius VII said he would do it only if he himself did the _____ as well as the anointing to show that the _____ power of the Church was supreme over the _____ power of the state.

g. Napoleon wanted his wife, _____, to be crowned empress.

h. Pius VII said Napoleon and his wife had to be _____ in the Church or he would not do the coronation.

i. Napoleon's coronation took place on December 2, _____, in the cathedral of _____ _____.

j. Pius VII first performed the ancient rite of _____, placing the holy _____ on Napoleon's head and each of his hands.

k. Napoleon's crown was an exact replica of the one _____ had worn at his coronation.

l. As the pope was getting ready to remove the crown from its cushion and place it on Napoleon's head, Napoleon stepped forward, seized the crown, and placed it slowly _____.

m. Napoleon then crowned _____.

n. Napoleon became the _____-anointed _____ of France, but Pope Pius VII was troubled that Napoleon had wrested from the Church her ancient right to crown _____ and _____.

Did you know? In the picture to the left, Napoleon is wearing a gold laurel crown. In Ancient Greece, wreaths of bay laurel (an evergreen) were used to crown the winner of a competition, such as the Olympics, or to honor a student who became a master in learning. Later it was used to crown the victors of war. Since the emperor or caesar of the Roman Empire was a military commander, the Roman Emperor wore a laurel wreath for his crown.

Napoleon had two crowns made for his coronation - the laurel crown and a more elaborate medieval-style crown (pictured to the right). The latter was much simpler than many royal crowns since it was not decorated with any diamonds or other precious jewels. This crown rested only briefly on Napoleon's head and then the empress's head during the actual coronation, and then Napoleon donned the laurel crown. When the Bourbon family returned to the throne of France, Napoleon's laurel crown was melted down. The "Crown of Napoleon I" is at the Louvre museum in Paris.

What message was Napoleon sending with his use of two crowns?

Chapter 8: **The Wars of Napoleon**

1. *In each statement below <u>cross out</u> the ending phrase that would make the statement <u>false</u>. (pgs. 205 – 207)*

a. Aleksandr I became tsar and emperor of Russia…

> … after his father, Tsar Pavel I, abdicated.
> … following the murder of his father.
> … when he was 23 years old.
> … in 1801.

b. The education of Aleksandr I had been influenced by…

> … his grandmother, Katerina the Great
> … his father, Tsar Pavel.
> … Swiss revolutionary, Frédéric César de La Harpe.
> … the enlightenment ideas of Rousseau.

c. During his reign, Aleksandr helped the Russian people by…

> … establishing schools, military academies, and new universities.
> … encouraging the growth of trade and manufacturing.
> … easing the burdens placed on the serfs.
> … making the censorship of books and periodicals stricter.

d. During his reign, Tsar Aleksandr…

> … made peace with Great Britain.
> … modernized Russia's army and navy.
> … expelled all foreigners from Russia.
> … increased the size of the Russian army by conscription.

e. Tsar Aleksandr decided to fight France because…

> … he thought Napoleon was a tyrant.
> … Napoleon wanted to depose Aleksandr as emperor.
> … Russia had a close relationship with Great Britain.
> … William Pitt promised him great sums of money.

f. The "Third Coalition" was…

> … the name of the new Russian constitution.
> … an alliance between Great Britain, Russia, and Austria.
> … formed to overthrow the power of Napoleon Bonaparte.
> … arranged by Prime Minister William Pitt.

2. *Use these words to complete the definitions below:* **abdicates, censorship, coalition, conscripts, deposed**

a. A _____ is a union of different groups for a common purpose.

b. A government _____ or drafts men when it forces them to join the military.

c. A king _____ when he voluntarily gives up his throne.

d. A king is _____ when he is forced to give up his throne.

e. A government practices _____ when it forbids the publication of materials it thinks is bad or dangerous.

3. *Answer the following questions. (pgs. 207 – 208)*

a. What amazed Daru about Napoleon's battle plans? _____

_____

b. Who did Napoleon think was the source of all his troubles in Europe?_____

4. *Number the events in the order they happened. (pgs. 207 – 211)*

a. _____ General Mack surrenders to Napoleon.

b. _____ Napoleon scraps his plan to invade England.

c. _____ On December 2, 1805, the armies meet in battle at Austerlitz.

d. _____ The *Grand Armée* moves swiftly into Germany and surrounds the Austrians under Genera Mack at Ulm.

e. _____ Napoleon learns that Admiral Villeneuve cannot sail the French fleet into the English Channel.

f. _____ Napoleon pursues his enemies, encamps, and prepares his men for battle with the Austrians and Russians.

g. _____ Napoleon dictates his detailed battle plans against the alliance to his secretary.

h. _____ The Third Coalition breaks up and Emperor Franz II signs a peace treaty with Napoleon.

i. _____ The Russians escape north and join forces with the Austrians near Brünn.

j. _____ Napoleon forces the Russians under General Kutuzov to retreat beyond Vienna.

k. _____ Under Napoleon's military genius, the French defeat the Russian and Austrian forces at Austerlitz.

l. _____ Fredrich Wilhelm of Prussia agrees to join the coalition but betrays his allies in a secret deal with Napoleon.

5. *Match the columns. (pgs. 207 – 211)*

A. Admiral Villeneuve	[ ] Napoleon greatest victory; defeat of the Third Coalition
B. William Pitt	[ ] commander of the Russian army
C. Friedrich Wilhelm III	[ ] great sea battle where the British defeated the French and Spanish
D. Franz II	[ ] capital of Austria
E. Kutuzov	[ ] commander of the French fleet
F. Karl Mack	[ ] another name for the Battle of Austerlitz
G. Queen Luise	[ ] commander of the English fleet in the battle against the French and Spanish
H. Vienna	[ ] king of Prussia
I. Battle of Austerlitz	[ ] peace treaty between Austria and Napoleon
J. Spain	[ ] commander of the Austrian army
K. Battle of Trafalgar	[ ] France's ally against Great Britain
L. Horatio Nelson	[ ] Prime Minister of England
M. England	[ ] Austrian Emperor
N. Battle of the Three Emperors	[ ] greatest sea power in the world
O. Treat of Pressburg	[ ] wife of Friedrich William of Prussia who encouraged her husband to join the coalition against Napoleon

6. *Finish this famous quote of Lord Nelson. (pg. 209)*

" _____ *expects every man to do his* _____."

Did you know? Did you notice something odd about this statue of Lord Nelson? Where is his right hand? In 1797, Nelson's right arm was amputated after a musket ball hit it. It is claimed that 30 minutes after the operation by the ship's surgeon, Lord Nelson was again giving commands to his men. In a previous battle, Nelson lost his sight in his right eye. Admiral Horatio Lord Nelson is one of Britain's great military heroes.

7. *Fill in the blanks to complete the problems between Napoleon and Pope Pius VII. (pgs. 211 – 212)*

a. Napoleon tried to _____ the Italian Church without consulting the pope.

b. Pope Pius refused to _____ the marriage of Napoleon's brother, Jerome Bonaparte.

c. Pope Pius would not side with Napoleon against _____.

d. Napoleon claimed _____ belonged to him.

e. Pope Pius would not acknowledge Napoleon as Roman _____.

f. Napoleon seized the Kingdom of _____ and made Joseph Bonaparte _____.

g. Napoleon wanted to _____ the pope's government.

h. Napoleon wanted to take all the Papal _____ for himself.

8. *In each statement below <u>cross out</u> the ending phrase that would make the statement <u>false</u>. (pgs. 212 – 213)*

a. The Confederation of the Rhine …

    … was an alliance between Napoleon and certain German states.

    … was a violation of the Franz II's rights as Holy Roman Emperor.

    … gave Napoleon supreme power.

    … was made of 16 German states that formally left the Holy Roman Empire.

b. The title of Holy Roman Emperor…

    … was ancient and venerable.

    … was coveted by Napoleon.

    … was an Enlightenment ideal.

    … belonged by right to the Habsburg family.

c. The Holy Roman Empire…

    … united Europe into Christendom.

    … began with Charlemagne.

    … ended on August 6, 1806.

    … was 2,000 years old.

9. Explain what Franz II did to keep Napoleon from becoming Holy Roman Emperor: *(pg. 213)*

_____

_____

_____

10. *Circle the correct word or phrase is bold that completes each sentence. (pg. 214)*

a. In 1806, Prussia, Russia, and Great Britain formed the **[Fourth Coalition/Continental System]** against Napoleon.

b. Even though the **[Russians/Prussians]** were disciplined and brave fighters, Napoleon defeated them at the Battles of Jena and Auerstädt.

c. Napoleon captured Berlin, the capital of **[Prussia/Russia]**.

d. Napoleon was certain **[England/Russia]** and its wealth was his real enemy.

e. The British naval **[confederation/blockade]** kept supplies from entering French ports.

e. Napoleon hoped his Berlin Decrees would ruin England's **[navy/economy]**.

f. Napoleon's Continental System tried to keep European countries from **[importing/exporting]** British goods.

11. *Number these events in the order they happened. (214 – 215)*

a. _____ Napoleon forced the Russians to retreat but suffered heavy casualties in the hard-fought battle.

b. _____ As Napoleon passed through Poland, thousands of Poles joined the Grand Armée to fight the Russians.

c. _____ On June 14, 1807 at Friedland, the French and Russians again met in battle.

d. _____ A month later, Napoleon, Aleksandr I, and Fredrich Wilhelm met in Tilsit to negotiate a peace treaty.

e. _____ Napoleon moved his army from Berlin towards Russia.

f. _____ The Russians engaged the French in battle at Eylau in February 1807.

g. _____ Instead of pursuing the enemy, Napoleon put into winter quarters.

h. _____ Even though the Russians put up a brave defense, the battle was a brilliant victory for Napoleon.

12. *Answer the following. (pgs. 215 – 216)*

a. What treaty ended the war between Napoleon and the Fourth Coalition? _____

b. Explain what each of the following countries lost or gained in this treaty.

Prussia: _____

_____

Russia: _____

_____

Poland: _____

_____

_____

c. What did Napoleon and Aleksandr pledge to each other in their secret treaty?

_____

_____

_____

13. *True or false? (pg. 217)*

a. _____ Napoleon wanted Pope Pius VI to obey him.

b. _____ The French bishops criticized Napoleon for being disrespectful to the pope.

c. _____ The bishops did whatever Napoleon wanted.

d. _____ The bishops and clergy demanded that all Frenchmen show Napoleon absolute obedience.

e. _____ The French bishops demanded Napoleon respect the Church's rights.

f. _____ Napoleon thought the Church should be more involved in politics.

g. _____ The Feast of the Assumption was replaced by St. Napoleon's Day in France.

h. _____ Priests who displeased Napoleon were imprisoned.

i. _____ The French bishops and clergy condemned Napoleon's wars.

j. _____ The bishops forbade Frenchmen from joining Napoleon's army.

k. _____ Napoleon thought the Church should only concern itself with spiritual matters.

14. What was the response to each of these requests or actions? (pg. 217)

a. Napoleon: "Declare war on Great Britain"

Pope Pius: _____

b. Napoleon; "Close your ports to English trade."

Pope Pius: _____

c. Pope Pius: "Come to Rome so we can talk face to face."

Napoleon: _____

d. Napoleon: "You must choose one-third of the cardinals from the French empire."

Pope Pius: _____

Napoleon: _____

e. General Miollis: "I have arrested the papal secretary of state and sent him away from Rome."

Pope Pius: _____

15. What was the main purpose of General Miollis' actions as military governor of Rome? (pg. 217)

_____

_____

Did you know? The Quirinal Palace is named after the hill on which it was built. Rome is built on seven hills east of the Tiber River and Quirinal Hill is the highest. The ancient Romans built a temple to the pagan god Quirinus on this hill and wealthy Romans built luxurious villas there as well. In the 16th century, Pope Gregory XIII decided to have a papal palace built there. Until then, the popes lived at the Lateran Palace on the Caelian Hill, closer to the Tiber. In the 19th century, the Quirinal became the royal residence of the King of Italy and, in the 20th century, the residence of the President of the Italian Republic. This palace is 20 times larger than the U.S. White House and has 1,200 rooms.

16. *Match the columns. (pgs. 217 – 218)*

A. Carlos IV   [   ] Duke of Wellington; commander of the British army

B. Manuel de Godoy   [   ] capital of Spain

C. Fernando VII   [   ] French general who led the French army into Spain and Portugal

D. Joseph Bonaparte   [   ] capital of Portugal

E. Fernando IV   [   ] brother of Napoleon who was made king of Spain by Napoleon

F. Jean-Andoche Junot   [   ] Prime Minister of Spain under Carlos IV

G. Joachim Murat   [   ] King of Spain from 1788 to 1808, cousin of Louis XVIII of France

H. Arthur Wellesley   [   ] King of Naples in Italy until 1808

I. Lisbon   [   ] son of Carlos IV who forced his father to abdicate

J. Madrid   [   ] married to Napoleon's sister; made king of Naples by Napoleon

17. *Number the events in the order they occurred. (pgs. 218 – 219)*

a. _____ The Spanish people rise in rebellion against Joseph Bonaparte and force him to flee Madrid.

b. _____ Napoleon decides to gain entire control of the Iberian Peninsula by getting rid of the Bourbon family.

c. _____ Napoleon keeps Carlos and Fernando in France and makes Joseph Bonaparte king of Spain.

d. _____ A British and Spanish army force the French to surrender at Andalusia.

e. __1_ The French army arrives in Portugal to punish the king for not closing his ports to British ships.

f. _____ Once in the Spanish capital, Napoleon issues decrees and commands the Spaniards to lay down their arms.

g. _____ The Spanish patriots push the French out of Saragossa.

h. _____ Crown Prince Fernando of Spain leads a successful uprising against his father and becomes king of Spain.

i. _____ The Duke of Wellington forces Junot to surrender Portugal and return to France.

j. _____ Napoleon "convinces" Carlos and Fernando to both abdicate and give him the Spanish throne.

k. _____ Learning of serious problems in France, Napoleon returns to Paris, leaving Spain in rebellion.

l. _____ Napoleon takes charge of the war in Spain and fights his way to Madrid.

m. _____ The Spanish refuse to submit to Napoleon and continue to fight for their king and their Catholic religion.

18. *Label these locations on the map: (pg. 219)*

> **Atlantic Ocean**
> **Mediterranean Sea**
> **France**
> **Portugal**
> **Spain**
> **Africa**
> **Lisbon**
> **Madrid**

19. *Fill in the blanks. (pgs. 220 – 222)*

a. Napoleon came back to France because he suspected _____, his former minister of foreign affairs was plotting against him.

b. Napoleon insulted and threatened _____, saying "You deserve that I should smash you like a _____. I can do it, but I _____ you too much to take the trouble."

c. In the spring of 1809, _____ and _____ formed the Fifth Coalition against Napoleon.

d. Napoleon beat the _____ in battle after battle and by May 13 was master of _____.

e. On May 17, Napoleon decreed that the pope no longer deserved to _____ because he had abused his _____ authority.

f. Napoleon took control of the _____ States and joined them to the _____ Empire.

g. Pope Pius VII responded by _____ Napoleon for violating the _____ of the Church.

h. When Napoleon sent French troops to the papal palace, the pope ordered the Swiss guards not to _____.

i. Pope Pius refused to _____ and was taken by the French troops into _____.

20. Explain the results of the Fifth Coalition's war against Napoleon: *(pg. 223)*

_____

_____

_____

_____

21. Write a word or phrase to describe Andreas Hofer and his life in each box. *(pgs. 224 – 225)*

Did you know? The official anthem of the Austrian Tyrol is a folk song about Andreas Hofer's death. The song *Zu Mantua in Banden* ends with the words "Farewell, my land Tyrol; farewell, my land Tyrol!"

22. *In each statement below* <u>cross out</u> *the ending phrase that would make the statement* <u>*false*</u>. *(pgs. 226 – 227)*

a. Napoleon's ambitions were…

> … to save the political and social reforms of the French Revolution.
> … to gain absolute power.
> … to make Europe more Catholic.
> … to reunite Europe into an empire of peace and justice.

b. Napoleon thought the Church should…

> … be free and independent in the empire.
> … be ruled by the emperor, not the pope.
> … have its center in Paris, not Rome.
> … teach people to obey and serve the emperor.

c. A hindrance to Napoleon's dream was…

> … the pope.
> … the rebellion in Spain.
> … Great Britain.
> … the Continental System.

d. To control all his conquered lands, Napoleon…

> … demanded that Frenchmen lay aside everything to fight and die for him.
> … became more democratic.
> … needed a standing army of one million men.
> … instituted a harsh and burdensome draft.

23. *Answer the following. (pgs. 277 – 228)*

a. Why did Napoleon divorce Josephine? _____

b. Why did Napoleon think this was an important reason to divorce her? _____

_____

c. What did the Church think about Napoleon's divorce? _____

_____

d. Whom did Napoleon marry in 1810? _____

e. Whose daughter was she? _____

f. Why did Napoleon's second marriage drive another wedge between him and the Church?

_____

_____

_____

_____

e. What event occurred on March 20, 1811 that made Napoleon and France rejoice?

_____

f. Who was given the title "King of Rome"?

_____

24. *Complete the following. (pgs. 228 – 229)*

a. Circle the names of the **three** men who were scheming against Napoleon's empire:

Pope Pius VII   Talleyrand   Metternich of Austria   Cardinal Consalvi   Tsar Aleksandr I

b. Underline **four** reasons Aleksandr I was becoming less friendly towards Napoleon:

He did not want to take second place to Napoleon.
He was angry that Napoleon had not married his daughter.
He feared Napoleon might exert his power over Russia
He thought Napoleon might reestablish an independent Polish kingdom.
Napoleon had broken the Treaty of Tilsit.
They both wanted to control Constantinople.

c. Underline **three** complaints Napoleon had against Tsar Aleksandr:

The tsar was Russian Orthodox instead of Catholic.
The tsar did not fully enforce the blockade against Great Britain.
The tsar formed an alliance with the Ottoman Empire.
The tsar did not help Napoleon in his war against Austria.
The tsar opened Russian ports to ships sailing under neutral flags.

d. Underline **four** descriptions of the *Grand Armée* gathered at the Nieman River:

It was a multinational army.
Frenchmen were conscripted into the army.
It was poorly equipped.
It numbered over one million men.
It was preparing to invade Russia.

25. *Label the map with the following locations:* ***French Empire, Russian Empire, Great Britain, Austrian Empire, Prussia, Spain, Paris, Moscow, London, Berlin, Vienna.*** *Outline the* ***Niemen River*** *and label it. (See maps on pgs. 226 and 230 in textbook.)*

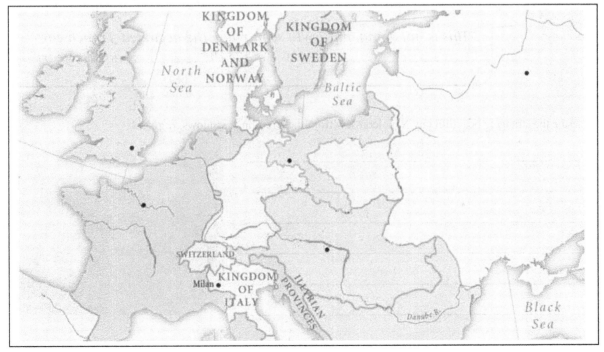

26. What were Tsar Aleksandr's words to the Russians after Napoleon's *Grand Armée* crossed into Russian territory in June of 1812? *Fill in the blanks. (pg. 229)*

"*Soldiers, you defend your _____, your _____, and your _____! I am with you. _____ is against the aggressor.*"

27. *Number the events in the order they happened. (pgs. 229 – 231)*

a. _____ The Russians retreat eastward, leaving Smolensk to Napoleon.

b. _____ The Russian army under General Barclay de Tolly retreats east.

c. _____ Kutuzov replaces Barclay de Tolly as commander of the Russian army.

d. _____ After tremendous losses on both sides, Kutuzov withdraws from the field of battle with his army still intact.

e. __1__ The *Grand Armée* advances into Russian territory to the Polish city of Vilna.

f. _____ Kutuzov decides to abandon Moscow to Napoleon and retreats with the army.

g. _____ The Russian peasants burn their villages and flee to the forests.

h. _____ In the march to Moscow, Napoleon loses thousands of men to hunger, illness, and guerilla attacks by Russians.

i. _____ Since the Russian army would not come out to fight, Napoleon storms Smolensk on August 17.

j. _____ On September 7, Kutuzov engages Napoleon in a bloody battle at Borodin, 71 miles west of Moscow.

k. _____ Barclay de Tolly's forces join up with General Bagration's forces at Smolensk.

l. _____ Instead of wintering in Smolensk, Napoleon decides to march on Moscow.

28. Fill in the blanks to complete Kutuzov's words as he made the decision to abandon Moscow. *(pg. 231)*

"*Russia is not _____ as long as the _____ survives.*"

"*This is my doing, but I will soon make the accursed French eat _____, as I made the _____ do last year!*"

29. Describe the strangely beautiful city Napoleon saw from the Kremlin's windows. *(pg. 232)*

_____

_____

_____

_____

_____

_____

30. *Number the events in the order they happened. (pgs. 231 – 233)*

a. _____ On October 19, the *Grand Armée* retreats from Moscow with the spoils of the city.

b. _____ Napoleon enters an empty and silent Moscow on September 16, 1812.

c. _____ The destruction of Moscow leaves Napoleon's army without food or fuel to survive the Russian winter.

d. _____ Napoleon reaches the Berezina River and discovers the supplies he ordered gathered are not there.

e. __1__ The 200,000 residents of Moscow flee with their possessions.

f. _____ The Grand Armée finally crosses the Niemen River and into safety on December 14, 1812.

g. _____ Tsar Alexandr vows he will never surrender to the French.

h. _____ Napoleon pushes on to the Niemen River with his army a confused mass of broken men.

i. _____ On the evening of Napoleon's entry into Moscow, fires break out and the city begins to burn.

j. _____ The soldiers of the *Grand Armée* destroy churches and homes, and loot and pillage Moscow.

k. _____ On Nov. 11, Napoleon reaches Smolensk and as he is leaving he orders its walls and towers to be blown up.

l. _____ Napoleon receives disturbing news from Paris and abandons his army on December 6 to return to France.

31. Write **four** reasons why the retreat from Moscow devastated Napoleon's army: *(pgs. 232 – 233)*

- _____
  _____
- _____
  _____
- _____
  _____
- _____
  _____

32. *Answer the following. (pgs. 232 – 233)*

a. Napoleon led 400,000 troops into Russia. How many did he have by the time he left Moscow? _____

b. How many of his troops returned to the encampment at the Niemen River?_____

c. Were more troops lost on the march <u>to Moscow</u> or on the retreat <u>from Moscow</u>? _____

d. How many men did Napoleon lose altogether in his six months in Russia? _____

e. What percentage of the army was lost in the Russian campaign? _____

Did you know? Napoleon's doomed Russian campaign inspired works of art. The book *War and Peace* is a historical novel about Napoleon's invasion of Russia. It was published by Russian author Leo Tolstoy in 1869. The main characters are aristocrats and military men from Moscow and the story vividly portrays the drama of Napoleon's invasion. The Russian composer Tchaikovsky wrote the *1812 Overture* to commemorate Russia's defense against the French invaders. It has a very dramatic finale which includes the sound of cannon fire – sometimes done outdoors with real cannons (with blanks), but usually imitated by drums. It is a very stirring piece and is often played to accompany fireworks at 4th of July celebrations.

33. What disturbing news did Napoleon receive from France while he was retreating from Moscow? Fill in the blanks to complete part of the letter he may have received. *(pg. 233)*

> ...*spread the news that you had been* _____ *in Russia. The senate has proclaimed a* _____. *The conspirators have imprisoned the prefect of* _____ *and taken control of Paris'* _____.
>
> *I fear it is* _____!
>
> *You must come at once to save your* _____ *and the lives of the* _____ *and your* _____.

Extra Credit

Napoleon was a brilliant general and had been unconquerable until his Russian campaign. Why do you think he made the fatal mistake of marching on Moscow?

Chapter 9: Metternich's Europe

1. *Complete the following. (pg. 238)*

a. Underline **two** reasons Tsar Aleksandr was determined to bring Napoleon down:

> Napoleon's army had devastated Russia.
> Tsar Alexander wanted to rule France.
> He thought Napoleon was the enemy of God and man.

b. Circle the countries that joined Russia in the Sixth Coalition against Napoleon:

Great Britain   Austria   Sweden   Prussia   Italy

c. Circle the name of the man who discouraged his country from joining the coalition:

Pope Pius VII   Friedrich Wilhelm III   Prince Metternich

d. Underline **two** reasons Germans formed the *Tugendbund*:

> They resented French rule and wanted to drive the French from their homeland.
> The league had to be secret because their government was controlled by Napoleon.
> They had secret plans to rescue Pope Pius VII.

e. Underline **three** descriptions of other parts of Napoleon's empire:

> They wanted Tsar Aleksandr to be emperor instead of Napoleon.
> They did not want to be pawns of a foreign ruler.
> They wanted national independence.
> They did not want to be ruled by a tyrant.

2. *On the map below, circle the places where Napoleon won four battles against the Sixth Coalition in 1813. Draw an X next to the place where Napoleon suffered a massive defeat in the Battle of the Nations in October 1813. (pgs. 239 – 240)*

3. *Complete the following (pg. 241)*

a. Why did Napoleon want to make peace with the Church?

_____

_____

b. Even though Pope Pius VII was reluctant, why did he sign the new concordat?

_____

_____

c. Which of the following was an agreement contained in the new concordat?

      The pope had to live at Paris.

      Napoleon could have more authority over the bishops in his domain.

      Secular rulers could nominate two-thirds of the cardinals.

d. Why did Pope Pius VII later repudiate the concordat? _____

_____

e. What did Napoleon do in response to the pope's rejection of the concordat?

_____

_____

4. *Number the events in the order they occurred. (pgs. 241 – 242)*

a. ____ Tsar Aleksandr leads his army to Paris and "liberates" the city.

b. _1_ Napoleon returns to Paris in defeat from the Battle of Leipzig.

c. ____ Napoleon is allowed to keep the title of emperor and sent to the small island of Elba to rule.

d. ____ Louis XVIII enters Paris to take up the throne of his ancestors.

e. ____ The king of Naples betrays Napoleon and sends 30,000 troops to the allies.

f. ____ One of Napoleon's oldest and most trusted generals deserts with part of the army to the enemy.

g. ____ The British and Spanish forces drive the French from Spain and enter southern France.

h. ____ The coalition decides to invade France and crosses the Rhine River.

i. ____ Even though he is greatly outnumbered, Napoleon almost drives the allies from France.

j. ____ On April 11, 1814 Napoleon surrenders and abdicates.

5. *Match the columns. (pgs. 239 –*

A. subsidy   [ ] knot of white ribbon; symbol of loyalty to the French monarchy

B. Klemens von Metternich   [ ] brother of Louis XVI, heir to the throne of France

C. House of Bourbon   [ ] reject

D. Battle of the Nations   [ ] money given by a government to another government, group, or person

E. white cockade   [ ] minister of foreign affairs for Austria

F. repudiate   [ ] blue, white and red symbol of the French revolution

G. Louis Stanislas   [ ] ruling family of France overthrown in the French Revolution

H. tricolor flag   [ ] battle at Leipzig between Napoleon and the multinational coalition army

6. *Complete the following. (pgs. 243 - 244)*

a. Check the experiences and influences that made Metternich a foe of liberal revolution and a defender of monarchy:

    ____ Revolutionary violence had forced him to leave the University of Strasbourg when he was 17.

    ____ He had witnessed the beheading of King Louis XVI by the revolutionaries.

    ____ French *émigrés* told him lurid tales of revolutionary violence.

    ____ He met the future King George IV in England.

    ____ Napoleon had killed his father, a diplomat of the Austrian court.

    ____ He married the granddaughter of Empress Maria Theresia's chancellor.

b. Fill in the blanks to complete Metternich's thoughts on government:

    Princes, not _____ assemblies should direct society.

    Legitimate monarchs make governments _____ and _____.

    Democracies and republics become _____.

c. Check the characteristics of the Concert of Europe:

    ____ It was a plan formed by Metternich to make Austria the most powerful nation in Europe.

    ____ It was a plan to assure peace and stability in Europe.

    ____ It was a plan to make sure Napoleon stayed on Elba.

    ____ It would punish France for supporting Napoleon's regime.

    ____ It would hold periodic gatherings of representatives from the European nations.

    ____ It would settle disputes between nations.

    ____ It would work to suppress revolutionary movements.

    ____ It would make Louis XVIII the new Holy Roman Emperor.

d. On what date did the Congress of Vienna officially meet? _____

e. The following powers sent delegates to the Congress of Vienna. Circle the **four** powers that controlled the Congress.

Portugal   Great Britain   Austria   Sweden   Spain   Prussia   Germany   France   Russia

f. Write the power that each of these men represented at the Congress:

    Lord Castlereagh   _____

    Metternich   _____

    Prince von Hardenburg   _____

    Tsar Aleksandr I   _____

    Talleyrand   _____

    Cardinal Consalvi   _____

g. Underline the names of the men above who decided they would make all the decisions for Europe.

h. What was the attitude of the delegates toward the Church? _____

_____

i. What happened in March 1815, that upset the Congress of Vienna's plans?

_____

_____

7. *Use these words in the sentences below:* ***concert, despotism, legitimate, delegate, stability, balance of power***

a. Louis XVIII was the _____ monarch of France because he was a member of the Bourbon family.

b. Keeping the same government and laws helps give _____ to a country.

c. A _____ exists when one nation cannot make other countries do what it wants.

d. A _____ is a person who represents a country or group of people.

e. A _____ is held when people join together to do something.

f. A democracy becomes a _____ when the people are controlled by a tyrant.

8. *In each statement below* <u>cross out</u> *the ending phrase that would make the statement false. (pgs. 245 -247)*

a. As Napoleon landed in France and proceeded to Paris…

> … joyous crowds welcomed him.
> … he overcame opposition without fighting.
> … he won battle after battle.
> … King Louis XVIII fled from Paris.

b. Even though Napoleon was master of France again, he was not happy because…

> … royalists and Liberals were hatching plots against him.
> … he could not gather an army to fight the allies.
> … the Austrians refused to return his son to him.
> … his wife refused to ever see him again.

c. At the Battle of Waterloo…

> … Napoleon's reputation as an invincible commander was destroyed.
> … the Duke of Wellington led the allies to victory.
> … the Seventh Coalition rid Europe of Napoleon.
> … Napoleon was captured and imprisoned.

d. After his defeat at Waterloo, Napoleon…

> … tried to commit suicide.
> … thought about escaping to the United States.
> … abdicated to keep France from civil war.
> … sought refuge in England.

9. What was the date of the Battle of Waterloo? *(pg. 246)* _____

10. What did the British government decide to do with Napoleon? Give details. *(pg. 247)*

> "I ought to have died at Waterloo."

_____

_____

_____

_____

_____

Name _____ Date _____

11. *Circle the correct answer for each sentence. (pgs. 248 – 250)*

a. The meeting of European delegates in Austria in 1814 and 1815 was called the:

   Seventh Coalition   **Congress of Vienna**   **German Confederation**

b. The loose alliance of 38 German states that replaced the Holy Roman Empire was called the:

   Quadruple Alliance   **Holy Alliance**   **German Confederation**

c. The league that made sure European nations obeyed the decisions of the Congress of Vienna was the:

   Quadruple Alliance   **Seventh Coalition**   **German Confederation**

d. The league that made sure Liberal revolutions were kept down was the:

   Quadruple Alliance   **Holy Alliance**   **Treaty of Paris**

e. The Holy Alliance was the idea of:

   Metternich   **Pope Pius VII**   **Tsar Aleksandr**

f. The country that dominated the German Confederation and had the most votes was:

   Prussia   **Bavaria**   **Austria**   **Russia**

g. To make sure rulers acted according to Christian principles and ideals, European nations joined the:

   Holy Alliance   **Concert of Europe**   **Papal Peace Plan**

h. France and the major European powers agreed to the decisions of the Congress when they signed the:

   1815 Treaty of Paris   **Holy Alliance**   **1815 Indemnity Act**

i. The statesman responsible for negotiating the decisions of the Congress of Vienna was:

   Pope Pius VII   **King George III**   **Prince von Metternich**

j. The only one who took the Holy Alliance seriously was:

   Pope Pius VII   **Tsar Aleksandr**   **Prince George**

k. One of the chief guiding forces of European life in the first half of the 19th century was:

   the Holy Alliance   **Liberalism**   **nationalism**

12. Check the accomplishments of the Congress of Vienna. *(pgs. 248 – 250)*

   ____ The boundaries of the European states mostly returned to what they had been before the French Revolution.

   ____ Napoleon's son was made king of France.

   ____ Poland was given its independence.

   ____ The pope regained the Papal States.

   ____ The Holy Roman Empire was restored with Franz I as emperor.

   ____ European rulers regained the thrones they had lost to Napoleon.

   ____ The German states were formed into a new union.

   ____ Great Britain was forced to pay an indemnity to France.

   ____ Liberalism and revolution were suppressed.

13. Why did Liberals hate the Holy Alliance? *(pg. 250)* _____

_____

_____

14. Fill in the blanks to complete the description of Napoleon's government. *(pgs. 250 – 251)*

a. Napoleon preserved and spread the ideas of _____ during his reign.

b. He wanted to use his power to bring the ideals of _____, _____, fraternity, and the _____ of man to all Europe.

c. Because France's revolutionary governments were unstable and corrupt, Napoleon thought the only way to save the principles of the French Revolution was through _____.

d. When Napoleon was emperor, he abolished all privileges based on _____ or _____ status.

e. He wanted noblemen, churchmen, townsmen, and peasants to be _____ in the sight of the law.

f. In Napoleon's domains, _____ received no special privileges, state _____ were abolished, and Catholics, Protestants, and Jews were granted equal _____ rights.

g. He established a modern _____ state where government is independent of _____.

15. Write **four** characteristics of a modern state: *(pg. 251)*

➢ _____

➢ _____

➢ _____

➢ _____

16. Fill in the blanks to show how Napoleon made France a modern state. *(pg. 251)*

a. One _____ code was established for all of France.

b. A system of national _____ was formed for all French people.

c. All French men were required to do _____ service.

d. All persons had to treat France and the _____ as more _____ than anything else.

e. No special recognition or protection was given to any particular _____.

17. *Answer the following, (pg. 251)*

a. What was the old civilization or Christendom based on? _____

b. What was Napoleon's idea of a new "Christendom" based on? _____

c. What ideas spread throughout Europe because of Napoleon's conquests? _____

d. What ideal did Napoleon inspire in Europe that eventually overthrew his empire? _____

e. Did most Europeans defend their homelands because of love for their country or because of Liberal ideas?

_____

f. What is nationalism? _____

_____

g. Why did nationalism and Liberalism become inseparable ideas in the 19th century?

_____

_____

Name _____ Date _____

18. *In each statement below* <u>cross out</u> *the ending phrase that would make the statement* <u>*false.*</u> *(pgs. 252 – 254)*

a. Catholics and serious Christians rejoiced at the fall of Napoleon because…

> … he had destroyed the Holy Roman Empire.
> … he closed monasteries and persecuted faithful priests.
> … he did not respect the Church or the pope.
> … he had enacted anti-Christian policies.

b. Many Christians supported monarchy as the only true form of government because…

> … of the violence of the French Revolution and the Napoleonic wars.
> … Liberals supported democracy and promoted anti-Catholic policies.
> … the Church teaches that democracy or representative governments are immoral.
> … the ancient regime showed more respect to the Church, and the pope.

c. European rulers gained a new respect for religion because…

> … Europe was undergoing a religious revival.
> … the pope condemned democracy.
> … of the courage shown by Catholics and the pope during years of persecution.
> … a union of "throne and altar" could strengthen governing authority.

d. Many Europeans thought 25 years of rationalism and Enlightenment government had brought to Europe…

> … nothing but perpetual war and a shattered society.
> … bloodthirsty men and tyrants in place of the old nobles.
> … the loss of millions of lives.
> … new hope and stability.

19. Fill in the blanks to complete the different opinions on how to restore Europe. *(pg. 254)*

a. Metternich: "The ancient regime should be restored, as if the _____ never happened.

b. Tsar Aleksandr: "We should keep some _____ reforms, but the spirt of _____ should guide the dealings nations have with one another."

c. Schlegel: "Things should be as they were in the _____ when the Catholic Church had supreme authority. The _____ Empire should also be restored."

d. De Maistre: "We must have a new _____ age. It will be formed either by a new _____ or the renewed _____ Church."

20. What did Pope Pius VII do in 1814 that did not please European leaders? _____

_____

21. In each box, write a fact about Klemens Maria Hofbauer. *(pg. 253)*

22. *Answer the following. (pgs. 255)*

a. What did Metternich think needed to be eradicated to maintain peace in Europe? _____

b. What happened to nationalists in Austria's domains who called for independence for their people?

_____

c. How did Metternich keep the military from joining any rebellions in the Austrian Empire?

_____

d. Write **three** ways Metternich suppressed Liberal ideas in Austria:

➢ _____

➢ _____

➢ _____

23. Check the correct descriptions of the German Confederation. *(pgs. 255 – 256)*

_____ The German states were more conservative than Austria.

_____ Some of the German states modeled their laws after the *Code Napoleón*.

_____ City workers wanted more freedom to demand better working conditions.

_____ The middle class wanted the right to participate in government.

_____ It was controlled by the Austrian government.

_____ Many Germans wanted Germany to be united into one nation.

_____ Liberal ideas were strong in German universities.

_____ German professors tried to crush Liberal movements among their students.

24. *Fill in the blanks. (pg. 256)*

The _____ Decrees of 1819 were laws approved by the diet of the German Confederation that required the

government to supervise the _____ and the _____ and forbade any member state of

the confederation to adopt a constitution that was not _____ or was opposed to _____.

Through these decrees, Metternich was able to break the power and influence of _____ groups in Germany.

25. *Circle the correct word or phrase in **bold** that completes each sentence. (pg. 256 – 257)*

a. Louis XVIII did not try to restore the ancient regime to France because he (**believed and supported Liberal ideas/ was afraid he would lose his throne if he did).**

b. Louis XVIII (**preserved/eliminated**) France's constitutional monarchy and the *Code Napoleón*.

c. In the Bourbon government, the Catholic Church (**was/was not**) recognized as the state religion of France.

d. In the White Terror of 1815, (**Liberals/royalists**) attacked and killed (**Liberals/royalists**).

e. When (**Liberals/royalists**) gained control of France's legislature in 1815, they restricted freedom of (**the press/ religion**), established new courts to try treason, and abolished (**civil divorce/military service**).

f. In 1816, a moderate royalist legislature who (**was not/was**) willing to compromise with the Liberals was elected.

g. After a (**royalist/Liberal**) assassinated the king's nephew in 1820, a very (**royalist/Liberal**) majority was elected to the French legislature.

h. The new legislature (**increased/lessened**) the power of wealthy citizens over the government.

26. Check the characteristics of the Spanish Constitution of 1812. *(pg. 257)*

____ It was drawn up by Napoleon.

____ It gave most of the governmental power to a legislature.

____ It did not allow the king to make laws.

____ It allowed the king to veto or stop bills from becoming laws.

____ It granted freedom to all religions.

____ It declared the Catholic Faith as the official religion of Spain.

____ It allowed for freedom of the press, but publications were forbidden to attack the Catholic Faith.

____ It allowed the nobility and the Church to have representatives in the one-house legislature.

27. *Number the events in the order they occurred. (pgs. 257 – 258)*

a. ____ King Fernando took an oath to support the Constitution of 1812.

b. ____ When the Spanish ministers refused to obey the Quadruple Alliance, France sent an army into Spain.

c. ____ After the fall of Napoleon, Fernando VII regained his throne and abolished the new constitution.

d. ____ The *cortes*, with the king as their prisoner, fled south to Cádiz.

e. ____ In 1819 and 1820 rebellions broke out against the government throughout Spain.

f. __1__ In 1812 Spanish resistance leaders established a junta and drew up a new constitution.

g. ____ Fernando continued his brutal purge of Spain and broke the power of the Liberals.

h. ____ Fernando VII reigned as absolute monarch of Spain for five years.

i. ____ A Liberal *cortes* governed Spain while Fernando plotted to overthrow it.

j. ____ After the king promised to grant them a pardon, the revolutionaries released him and surrendered to the French.

k. ____ When Fernando regained power, he broke his word and arrested and executed the *cortes* and their supporters.

l. ____ In 1823, the Quadruple Alliance demanded that the Spanish government abolish the Constitution of 1812 and restore the king's powers.

28. *Answer the following. (pgs. 259 – 262)*

a. Explain what changes the Liberal groups in Italy wanted. _____

_____

_____

b. Write an important fact about the Carbonari in each box.

c. Explain why Liberalism was not popular with the majority of people in Spain and Italy.

_____

_____

_____

d. Give an example of how Pope Pius VII showed his spirit of forgiveness when he returned to Rome.

_____

_____

_____

e. What was the Pius VII's greatest gift to Napoleon? _____

f. Describe Napoleon's life in St. Helena:

_____

_____

_____

_____

_____

_____

_____

_____

_____

_____

g. In what way did the Pius VII conquer Napoleon? _____

_____

_____

h. Fill in the blanks to complete this quote of Napoleon:

"The power that rules over _____ has a greater power than that which rules over _____."

i. When did Napoleon die? _____

j. When did Pope Pius VII die? _____

k. During his reign as emperor, Napoleon considered Pope Pius VII and the Catholic Church as his rivals. Do you think he changed his mind at the end of his life? Explain your answer.

_____

_____

_____

Name _____ Date _____

Chapter 10: Romanticism and Revolt, Part I

1. Classic or Romantic? *If the statement below describes Romanticism, write "R". If the statement describes Classicism, write "C". (pgs. 265 – 269)*

a. _____ Artists copy the finite beauty of the natural world.

b. _____ Artists try to express infinite beauty and the unseen world.

c. _____ It was inspired by the spirit of the Middle Ages.

d. _____ It was inspired by the Enlightenment.

e. _____ It was a rejection of the whole Enlightenment.

f. _____ Artists have a great deal of freedom of expression.

g. _____ The literature and art of the ancient world are the ideal of beauty.

h. _____ Artists cannot deviate from certain strict rules.

i. _____ Art should express more than what is seen and experienced in everyday life.

j. _____ It imitates the Classical Greek and Roman spirit.

k. _____ It emphasizes reason, proportion, brilliance and wit.

l. _____ Artists look inside themselves rather than the outside world for inspiration.

2. *Complete the following. (pgs. 266 – 269)*

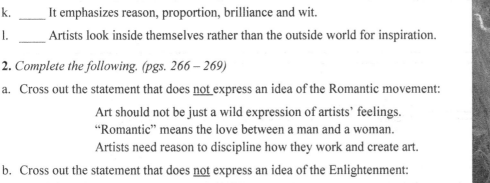

a. Cross out the statement that does <u>not</u> express an idea of the Romantic movement:

> Art should not be just a wild expression of artists' feelings.
> "Romantic" means the love between a man and a woman.
> Artists need reason to discipline how they work and create art.

b. Cross out the statement that does <u>not</u> express an idea of the Enlightenment:

> Human reason is the only judge of what is true, good, and beautiful.
> True knowledge only comes by experience and experiment.
> There are some things that cannot be grasped by the senses or reason alone.
> Religious faith is worthless and the supernatural is irrational

c. Cross out the statement that does <u>not</u> describe mysticism:

> The world contains mysteries that can only be grasped by an inner eye.
> Scientific methods and deductive reasoning are not the only source of knowledge.
> Everything perceived by the senses points to something greater and deeper than itself.
> It is rejected by the Catholic Faith
> Everything is an image or symbol of God.

d. Cross out the statement that does <u>not</u> explain why so many Romantics became Catholic:

> Major Protestant churches had become too rationalistic.
> The Catholic Church offered a mystical view of God and the universe.
> The Catholic Church had created medieval culture.
> The Catholic Church was against reason and science.

3. *Write two important facts about each of these Romantic movement characters. (pgs. 265 – 271)*

Friedrich von Schlegel

Novalis

Adam Heinrich Müller

Clemens Brentano

Ludwig van Beethoven

4. Write **two** <u>good</u> effects Romanticism had on European society: *(pg. 270)*

➢ _____

➢ _____

5. Write **two** <u>negative</u> effects Romanticism had on European society: *(pg. 270)*

➢ _____

➢ _____

Name _____ Date _____

6. *Fill in the blanks to complete the answer for each question. (pgs. 271 – 274)*

a. Why was Great Britain not influenced by the revolutionary ideas that had raged through the rest of Europe?

The English associated revolutionary ideas with _____, who was the enemy of England. Since England's _____ government was directing the war against _____, it made Englishmen more _____ to the government and they turned against anyone who was _____ the government or calling for _____. Because most Englishmen did not care about democratic government or want anything to drastically change, Great Britain remained an _____ where Parliament was controlled by the _____ and wealthy merchants.

b. Why did more English begin to question the status quo?

The years after the Battle of Waterloo were particularly hard on _____ in the cities and countryside. Periods of unprecedented economic _____ caused unemployment. Many people in the countryside were already were living in _____ because _____ had pushed them off the land and bad _____ meant even less work for them.

c. What conditions did William Cobbett witness in the countryside that caused him to fight for reforms?

Cobbett saw how badly the _____ revolution and the enclosures were affecting the poor. Peasants could not be secure or feed themselves because they were losing their _____ and prices for goods were rising because of the _____. Landlords were demanding shorter _____ and higher _____. When peasants could not afford to pay, they were _____. Financiers and speculators were taking advantage of farmers for quick _____.

d. How did William Cobbett fight for reform?

Cobbett wrote _____ attacking all the evils he saw in the English _____. He first published a weekly _____ called the *Political Register* and then an inexpensive _____ for workers called the *Register*.

e. What were some of the reforms that "radicals" in England were calling for?

Reformers wanted the "pocket" or "rotten" _____ to be abolished. They wanted the right to _____ to be extended to new _____ cities and to wider groups of people. They wanted members of Parliament to receive a _____ so others beside the rich could be members. They demanded an end to _____ and other forms of corruption.

f. What did Cobbett think would give Englishmen more freedom?

Cobbett thought as many people as possible needed to own _____, such as _____ and _____ for manufacturing goods. This would insure _____ was well-distributed or divided among all social _____.

g. What did Parliament do after the workers' riots in 1816?

Based on information from government _____, Parliament decided rioters wanted to _____ the "established government." With this excuse, Parliament suspended the right to _____ and _____ radical leaders.

7. Finish this quote by William Cobbett. *(pg. 274)*

"_____ means nothing else than the full and quiet enjoyment of your own _____. If you have not this; if this be not well secured to you, you may call yourself what you will, but you are a _____."

8. *Answer the following. (pgs. 274 – 275)*

a. Why were people gathered at St. Peter's Field on August 16, 1819?

_____

_____

_____

b. Describe what happened at the Peterloo Massacre.

_____

_____

_____

_____

_____

_____

c. What did Parliament do in response to the Peterloo Massacre?

_____

_____

9. *Circle the correct word in **bold** that completes each sentence.* (pgs. 276 – 277)

a. Since the 16th century Catholics were **(allowed/forbidden)** to be members of Parliament.

b. Catholics **(could/could not)** vote for members of Parliament.

c. Only **(Protestants/Catholics)** could serve as magistrates in Ireland.

d. Catholics **(were/were not)** required to pay tithes to support the Protestant Church of England.

e. In the 19th century, Catholics **(could/could not)** be fined or imprisoned for being Catholic in England.

f. King George IV **(supported/opposed)** any efforts for Catholic emancipation.

g. The Tory controlled Parliament **(supported/opposed)** government reforms.

h. In *The History of the Protestant Reformation in England*, Cobbett criticized the **(Reformation/Catholic Church).**

i. Cobbett claimed the life of the poor was **(better/worse)** since England became Protestant.

j. Prime Minster **(Canning/Wellington)** introduced the Catholic Relief Act of 1829 and it was passed by Parliament.

10. How did the Catholic Relief Act benefit Catholics? *(pgs. 276 – 277)*

_____

_____

11. How did the Catholic Relief Act keep the peasants of Ireland from voting? *(pg. 277)*

_____

_____

12. *Number the events in the order they happened. (pgs. 277 – 278)*

a. _____ The upper classes in England feared a "French Revolution" was happening in their country.

b. _____ In elections, the Tories lost seats to the Whigs in Parliament.

c. _____ King George IV died in 1830 and his brother came to the throne as King William IV.

d. _____ Workmen who had rioted were put on trial and about 450 men were exiled to British colonies overseas.

e. _____ Workmen's riots spread throughout England.

f. _____ The Duke of Wellington was forced to step down as prime minister.

g. _____ Lord Grey's government crushed the Last Laborers' Revolt with harsh measures.

h. _____ William IV appointed Charles, Earl Grey, as prime minister.

i. _____ Local magistrates could or would not put down the insurrections.

13. *In each statement below <u>cross out</u> the ending phrase that would make the statement <u>false</u>. (pgs. 277 - 278)*

a. Peasant laborers throughout England rose in revolt because…

        … the enclosures caused poverty and starvation.

        … King William IV was a worse king than George III.

        … new agricultural machines put men out of work.

        … farmers could not pay good wages because of high tithes and taxes.

b. The mobs of rioting English workmen…

        … murdered landlords and parsons.

        … destroyed threshing machines

        … met with the local landlords and farmers to demand their rightful pay.

        … burnt haystacks.

c. The British courts punished the rioting workmen by…

        … exiling them to British colonies overseas.

        … making them slaves.

        … separating them from their wives and children.

        … making them pay a benefice.

d. The proposed "home colonization" plan…

        … would divide unfarmed lands among propertyless laborers and their families.

        … would send workers to farm and make new homes overseas.

        … would help restore to peasants what they had lost under the enclosure movement.

        … was opposed by the aristocrats in Parliament.

Did you know? Great Britain might be a small island, but it had the largest empire in world history. Great Britain was a mighty naval power and this helped it establish colonies all over the world between the 16th and 18th centuries. It has had colonies on every continent. By the early 20th century the lands ruled by Great Britain covered almost 24% of the world. The mighty Roman Empire ruled only a little over 3% of the world's lands. The British Empire was described as "the empire on which the sun never sets" – meaning that it was always daylight in some part of its global empire. Can you find Great Britain on the map?

14. *Complete the following. (pgs. 278 – 280)*

a. Who supported Earl Grey's reform bill? Circle the correct answers.

King William IV	William Cobbett	Anglican bishops	House of Commons	House of Lords
aristocrats	industrialists	merchants	Lord Wellington	middle class

b. How was Earl Grey's reform bill passed? Fill in the blanks to complete the events.

- Earl Grey _____ the reform bill into Parliament in March 1931.
- The bill was defeated in the House of _____.
- King William _____ Parliament and called for new _____.
- A new House of _____ was elected and controlled by the _____ party.
- In September, a second reform bill passed the House of _____, but was defeated in the House of _____.
- In March 1932, a third reform bill was passed by the House of _____.
- Earl Grey asked the king to create new _____ who favored reform.
- The king refused and replaced Earl Grey with Lord _____ as prime minister.
- Strong opposition rose against _____'s government.
- The king made _____ prime minister and agreed to create new _____.
- Fearing that new _____ would give control to the Whig party, the House of _____ allowed the reform bill to pass.
- On June 7, 1932, William IV gave his royal _____ to the bill and it became law.

c. What changes were made because of the Reform Act of 1832? Check the correct statements.

___ Small towns and rotten boroughs gained seats in Parliament.
___ New industrial towns and cities gained seats in Parliament.
___ All Englishmen were given the right to vote for Parliament.
___ The lives of the urban poor and rural classes were improved.
___ The power and influence of businessmen and industrialists in government increased.
___ The Whigs gained control of Parliament.
___ The Tories became radical and fought for reform.
___ Parliament abolished black slavery throughout the British Empire.
___ Parliament removed cruel laws dealing with the imprisonment and punishment of criminals.
___ Parliament established a public health bureau.
___ The British government became more democratic and was not
      controlled by an oligarchy.

d. What reformer was elected to Parliament in 1832?

_____

e. After 1832, what was the new name of the Whig party?

_____

f. After 1832, what was the new name of the Tory party?

_____

Something to think about. The picture to the right is a political cartoon about the Reform Act of 1832. What do you think it means?

15. *Match the word to its definition. (pgs. 272 – 279) The definitions can be found in your textbook or a dictionary.*

A. depression   [   ] written statement that unjustly harms the reputation of another

B. peculation   [   ] disregard of the laws of morality; lack of self-control in one's behavior

C. fraud   [   ] being freed from the control or power of another

D. court-martial   [   ] to remove the right to vote from someone

E. libel   [   ] right that protects citizens from illegal imprisonment

F. financier   [   ] anything that encourages or promotes rebellion

G. speculator   [   ] the giving of money or valuable gifts to influence another's actions

H. enclosure   [   ] faithlessness or treachery

I. license   [   ] using lies or tricks to gain something unfairly or dishonestly

J. habeas corpus   [   ] lands and the wealth they produce, given as a grant to a member of the clergy

K. suffrage   [   ] one who deals with large amounts of money for investment

L. sedition   [   ] member of the British aristocracy – a duke, marquis, earl, viscount, or baron

M. repression   [   ] the fencing of all private lands off from common lands

N. emancipation   [   ] period of low business activity and production along with high unemployment

O. perfidy   [   ] the dishonest taking of money or property; embezzlement

P. disenfranchise   [   ] when a country establishes control over a foreign area by settling it

Q. benefice   [   ] trial of military persons by members of the military

R. bribery   [   ] the right to vote

S. peer   [   ] putting down by force.

T. colonization   [   ] one who buys property or goods to sell for a higher price than he bought them

16. *Complete the following. (pgs. 280 – 281)*

a. Describe how Tsar Aleksandr I changed during the latter years of his reign.

_____

_____

_____

_____

_____

b. Who succeeded Aleksandr as tsar? _____

c. Describe what happened in St. Petersburg on December 26, 1825. _____

_____

_____

_____

_____

_____

17. *Complete the following. (pg. 282)*

a. In each box, write a word or phrase that describes Tsar Nikolai I.

b. What were the three guiding principles of Nikolai's reign? _____

c. Write **three** ways Tsar Nikolai tried to protect Russians from non-Russian ideas:

➢ _____

➢ _____

➢ _____

d. Write **two** ways Tsar Nikolai tried to protect the Orthodox Church:

➢ _____

➢ _____

e. Complete this belief of Tsar Nicholas: To be Russian was to be _____.

18. *True or false? (pgs. 282 – 283)*

a. _____ The Ottoman Empire was ruled by Muslim Turks.

b. _____ The Ottoman Empire controlled the eastern part of the Mediterranean.

c. _____ The Turks had taken Greece from Russia in the 14th century.

d. _____ The Ottoman sultans freed the Greeks from oppression and poverty.

e. _____ Greece is on the Balkan Peninsula.

f. _____ The Greek people were happy under the rule of Ottoman sultans.

g. _____ The young sons of Orthodox Christians were forced to become Muslim.

h. _____ Orthodox Christians were sent to Siberia if they did not become Muslim.

i. _____ Young Greek men were drafted into the sultan's military guard.

j. _____ Under 500 years of Muslim rule, the Greek people became cruel and less civilized.

k. _____ The revolutions in western Europe inspired the Greeks to rise up and seek independence.

l. _____ The Greeks gathered a large, well-trained army to drive the Turks from their land.

m. _____ The Orthodox Archbishop Germanos did not support revolution against Muslim power and threatened to excommunicate anyone who fought in the revolution.

19. *Number the events in the order they happened. (pgs. 283 – 285)*

a. _____ European rulers sent aid and money to the insurgent Greek government.

b. _____ The revolt spread throughout Greece and soon the Turks were driven from Thessaly.

c. _____ Mahomet declared a jihad against Russia.

d. _____ On April 26, 1828, Russia declared war on the Ottoman Empire.

e. _____ By July 1827, it looked as if the Turks had destroyed the Greek revolution.

f. _____ In the spring of 1822, Mahomet II sent two Turkish armies to Greece to crush the revolt.

g. _____ When Mahomet refused, Russian and British fleets blockaded Morea, cutting off Ibrahim's supply line.

h. __1__ On April 2, 1821, Greek peasants in Morea revolted against the Turks and took the town of Patra.

i. _____ The great powers of the Concert of Europe met in London to decide what to do about the war in Greece.

j. _____ In 1824, Mahomet II sent Ibrahim Pasha with his fleet and army to Greece to end the rebellion.

k. __19_ On September 14, 1829, Russia and the Ottoman Empire signed the Treaty of Adrianople, ending the war.

l. _____ On April 22, the Ottoman Sultan, Mahomet II, murdered Patriarch Gregorios of Constantinople.

m. _____ France, Russia, and Great Britain pledged to make war on the sultan if he refused to make peace.

n. _____ The peasant leader, Kolokotrones and his army destroyed the Turks at Devernaki in the summer of 1822.

o. _____ While fighting the Turks, different Greek factions fought among themselves for leadership of the revolution.

p. _____ Tsar Nikolai I and Great Britain's prime minister tried to convince Mahomet to stop the war.

q. _____ Ibrahim conquered city after city, devastated the Greek countryside, and enslaved or slaughtered the Greeks.

r. _____ The Russians fought the Turks in Greece and freed Slavonic countries from Turkish rule.

s. _____ On October 20, 1827, a combined French, Russian, and British fleet destroyed the Turkish fleet in the Battle of Navarino.

20. *Complete the following. (pg. 285)*

a. Write **three** things Mahomet II agreed to in the Treaty of Adrianople:

➤ _____

➤ _____

➤ _____

b. What right did Nikolai I claim by the Treat of Adrianople? _____

_____

c. Fill in the blanks to complete the conditions of the treaty signed in London on May 7, 1832:

➤ Greece was declared a fully _____ state with _____ as its capital.

➤ The great powers of Europe chose the form of _____ Greece was to have.

➤ Greece was not to be a _____ as the rebels wanted, but a _____.

➤ Otto von Wittelsbach, the 17-year-old son of the king of _____ was made the first _____ of Greece.

➤ The great powers of Europe claimed the right to _____ in the affairs of Greece whenever they thought it was threatened by the _____ power in Constantinople.

21. *Using the map, complete the following: (pg. 287)*

a. Find and label these places: **Austria, Prussia, Russia, Warsaw**

b. Find **Poland**. Draw a line to show how it was roughly divided after the Congress of Vienna.

c. Label these places: **Congress Poland, Posen, Krakow**

d. Underline the names of the countries that divided Poland between themselves.

e. Circle the name of the country that controlled the largest part of Poland.

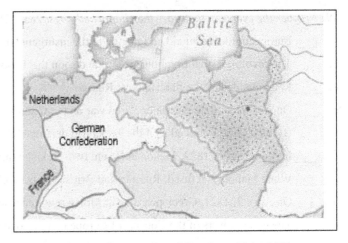

22. *In each statement below <u>cross out</u> the ending phrase that would make the statement <u>false</u>. (pgs. 286 – 287)*

a. Congress Poland was…

     … an independent kingdom with Russia's tsar as its king.

     … governed by a Russian imperial lieutenant.

     … a democratic republic with a constitutional monarchy.

     … a Catholic country, although it tolerated other religions.

b. The Poles rose up against Russian rule because…

     … secret police were used to suppress Polish patriotic movements.

     … the *Sejm* replaced Poles with Russians in the government and military.

     … the lieutenant governor was ignoring and violating the constitution.

     … Nikolai I was a harsh ruler and ignored Polish complaints.

c. The Polish Uprising of 1830 failed because…

     … the *Sejm* demanded unconditional surrender.

     … the revolutionaries were not united.

     … the Russian forces greatly outnumbered the revolutionaries.

     … the governments of Europe did not help the revolutionary cause.

d. After the end of the uprising, Tsar Nikolai…

     … abolished the government and constitution of Congress Poland.

     … made Congress Poland just another province of the Russian Empire.

     … made Russian the official language of the Polish government and courts.

     … executed all Poles who had fought in the rebellion.

23. Write **four** measures Nikolai I carried out against Catholics: *(pgs. 288 – 289)*

➢ _____

➢ _____

➢ _____

➢ _____

24. What effect did Nikolai's attempts to Russify Poland and Lithuania have? *(pg. 289)*

_____

_____

Chapter 11: **Romanticism and Revolt, Part II**

1. *Complete the following. (pgs. 293 – 294)*

a. How did Charles X differ from his brother Louis XVIII as king of France? _____

_____

_____

b. What did Charles X do that alarmed Liberals and angered Parisians? *Fill in the blanks:*

- He appointed _____ as his chief ministers.

- He payed _____ for the lands they had lost during the revolution.

- He restored _____ for women.

- He backed the "Law of _____."

- He disbanded the National _____.

- He permitted the _____ to return to France.

- He commanded the _____ of all journals and periodicals.

c. How did Charles X try to silence his opponents and fight for his rights as king of France? *Fill in the blanks:*

- He dissolved the French _____.

- He annulled the new _____.

- He removed the right to _____ from nearly three-fourths of the voters.

- He suspended the freedom of the _____.

d. What was the outcome of the king's actions? _____

_____

_____

2. *Match the columns. (pgs. 294 – 295) Some of the words are review terms.*

A. Louis XVI   [   ] grandson and heir of Charles X

B. Louis XVIII   [   ] aristocrats who fled France during the French Revolution

C. Charles X   [   ] Paris journalist who wrote against Charles X

D. Henri V   [   ] Duke of Orleans and cousin of Charles X; Liberal supporter

E. Adolphe Thiers   [   ] government with a king whose power is limited by a constitution

F. Jacques Lafitte   [   ] the middle class

G. Louis Philippe   [   ] king of France after Napoleon was overthrown

H. émigrés   [   ] government where citizens elect men to represent them

I. bourgeoisie   [   ] king of France who was executed during the French Revolution

J. republic   [   ] wealthy banker, supporter of Louis Philippe

K. constitutional monarchy   [   ] king who wanted to restore the ancient regime to France

3. *Complete the following. (pgs. 295 – 296)*

a. Write **two** reasons the bourgeoisie wanted a constitutional monarchy rather than a republic:

➤ _____

➤ _____

b. Why did the Liberals and bourgeoisie think Louis Philippe would be a good choice for a constitutional monarch?

_____

_____

_____

c. Explain how Louis Philippe became king.

_____

_____

_____

_____

4. Louis Philippe and Charles X seemed to be very different kings. *Read each phrase below. If it characterizes Louis Philippe, write **LP** on the line. If it characterizes Charles X, write **CX** on the line. If it describes both kings, write **both**. (pgs. 293 – 296)*

a. _____ House of Bourbon

b. _____ crowned and anointed in the cathedral at Reims

c. _____ King of the French

d. _____ enemy of the working class

e. _____ citizen king

f. _____ King of France

g. _____ lived like a wealthy bourgeois

h. _____ lived like a prince

i. _____ rich aristocrat

j. _____ Egalité

k. _____ lover of liberty

l. _____ His Most Christian Majesty

m. _____ tricolor flag

n. _____ authority comes from God

o. _____ authority comes from the people

p. _____ mingled with the rich and poor

q. _____ enemy of Liberals

r. _____ supporter of the French Revolution

s. _____ hated by the bourgeoisie

t. _____ ambitious politician

u. _____ deceptive

v. _____ faithful Catholic

w. _____ while lilies flag

x. _____ supported by royalists

5. What were Louis Philippe's real intentions in supporting Liberal ideals?

_____

_____

_____

_____

Name _____ Date _____

6. The Congress of Vienna united the Austrian Netherlands (Belgium) and the northern Netherlands (Holland) into one country, despite the two regions having very little in common. *List their differences below. (pgs. 296 – 297)*

	HOLLAND	**BELGIUM**
a. language	_____	_____
b. religion	_____	_____
c. economy	_____	_____
d. trade or imports	_____	_____
e. feelings towards the French	_____	_____

7. Why were the Belgians unhappy under the rule of Willem I? *Fill in the blanks. (pgs. 296 – 297)*

a. He forced them to follow _____ law and to use the _____ language.

b. He placed _____ officials over the Belgians.

c. He placed Belgian _____ under _____ ministers.

d. He attacked the _____ of the Catholic Church.

e. He proclaimed complete _____ freedom.

f. He forced Belgian businesses to pay high _____ to pay off Holland's heavy _____.

g. He favored free _____.

8. What were the results of the Belgian 1830 revolution against Willem I? *Check the true statements. (pg. 297)*

a. ____ Willem gave in to the demands of the rebels and the revolution ended without bloodshed.

b. ____ Metternich executed Willem for giving in to the rebels.

c. ____ Belgium became an independent country.

d. ____ Belgium got a new king but remained under the control of Holland.

e. ____ Belgium became an independent constitutional monarchy.

f. ____ Belgium became a democratic republic.

g. ____ Belgium's new constitution was based on Liberal ideas.

h. ____ Belgium's new constitution allowed freedom of religion and of the press.

i. ____ The new Protestant king, Leopold I, persecuted Catholics in Belgium.

9. *Answer the following questions. (pg. 297)*

a. How did the revolutionary spirit of 1830 influence Germany? _____

_____

_____

_____

_____

b. What ultimately had greater sway in Germany – the spirit of revolution or Metternich's theories of royal absolutism?

_____

_____

10. *Complete the following. (pgs. 298 – 299)*

a. Match the name of the ruler with the lands he/she ruled.

A. Francesco IV   [   ] Lombardy-Venezia

B. Franz I   [   ] Modena

C. Leopold II   [   ] Papal States

D. Carlo Felice   [   ] Parma

E. Maria Louisa   [   ] Piedmont-Sardinia

F. Fernando I   [   ] Sicily

G. Leo XII   [   ] Tuscany

b. On the map to the right, draw an "**H**" on the domains in Italy that were ruled by a member of the Habsburg family.

c. On the map to the right, circle the Italian states where there was peace and no Liberal rebellion.

d. On the map to the right, draw an "**X**" on the area where the suppression of rebellion was the most brutal.

11. Write two reasons Italians were discontent with the government of the Papal States: (pg. 299)

> _____

> _____

12. Write two reforms Pope Leo XII carried out during his reign: (pg. 299)

> _____

> _____

13. Write the name of the pope who matches each description. Underneath his name, write the years of his reign. *(pgs. 299 – 301)*

a. Pope _____: He reigned during the Napoleonic Era. After he excommunicated Napoleon, Napoleon had him imprisoned. Cardinal Consalvi was his competent and faithful secretary of state.

b. Pope _____: He did not support political reform. He thought the best way to fight Liberals was to defend the old ways and customs. He insisted on absolute obedience to constituted authority. His ministers used harsh measures against revolutionaries. He was greatly disliked by Italians of the middle class and the lower class.

c. Pope _____: During his short reign, he abolished the secret police established by his predecessor and recognized Louis Philippe as king of France. He decreed that the non-Catholic spouse in a mixed marriage must agree to the children being raised Catholic.

d. Pope _____: During his long reign, he faced two revolutions to overthrow the Papal States. Both were put down with the help of the Austrian army. He was in favor of minor political reforms in the Papal States, but fought the Liberals attempts to weaken his authority and to seize control of the government.

14. Give **three** examples that show how Pope Gregory XVI helped his people in the Papal States: *(pg. 302)*

➢ _____

➢ _____

➢ _____

15. Explain why Pope Gregory XVI had the reputation for being a reactionary. *(pg. 302)*

_____

_____

_____

_____

16. Explain why Pope Gregory XVI did not think there should be freedom to publish whatever one wanted to. *(pg. 302)*

_____

_____

_____

17. Write **three** beliefs condemned by Pope Gregory in his encyclical *Mirari Vos*: *(pg. 302)*

➢ _____

➢ _____

➢ _____

18. *Match the columns. (pgs. 301 – 304)*

A. reactionary

B. Centurions

C. indifferentism

D. Roman Question

E. *Mirari Vos*

F. *In Supremo Apostolatus*

G. Giuseppe Mazzini

H. *La Giovine Italia*

I. Massimo D'Azeglio

J. Carlo Alberto

[   ] "Young Italy" – a movement to inspire the youth of Italy to work for the freedom and unification of Italy

[   ] Pope Gregory XVI's apostolic letter condemning the slave trade

[   ] one who responds to an idea by taking the opposite opinion or reacts in an opposite manner

[   ] Italian painter and politician who promoted Italian liberation under a constitutional monarchy

[   ] Italian revolutionary who promoted the unification of Italy under a republican government.

[   ] what to do about the pope's temporal power in a united Italy

[   ] king of Piedmont-Sardinia in favor of Italian independence from Austria

[   ] belief that it makes no difference what religion one belongs to

[   ] Pope Gregory XVI's encyclical against the errors of Liberalism

[   ] group of irregular soldiers formed to combat Italian revolutionaries

Extra Credit: Metternich once said, "A Liberal pope is not a possible being." On a separate sheet of paper, explain the truth of this quotation. Make sure you define Liberalism (according to its use in the textbook) in your answer.

19. Write **three** reasons the French Liberals were disappointed with the reign of King Louis Philippe: *(pg. 304)*

➤ _____

➤ _____

➤ _____

20. Write **four** ways *laissez-faire* economic ideas affected European society: *(pg. 306)*

➤ _____

➤ _____

➤ _____

➤ _____

21. Which of the following are true statements about the Saint-Simonian ideas of social reform? *(pgs. 306 - 307)*

a. _____ The best way to bring about social reform is through violence.

b. _____ No individual or group should own private, productive property.

c. _____ The government should own all farms, shops, and factories.

d. _____ Productive property should be owned in common under the control of a group of industrial chiefs.

e. _____ Only scientists should have the right to vote.

f. _____ The Church should take care of the poor.

g. _____ Everyone should have the right to vote, even women.

h. _____ Women should be considered in every way equal to men.

i. _____ Scientists can direct society toward peace and prosperity better than the Church.

j. _____ Everyone in society should be absolutely equal in all things.

k. _____ Each person should be rewarded according to how much he or she contributes to society.

22. Fill in the blanks to complete the ideas of the socialist Louis Blanc. *(pg. 307)*

a.
> "To each according to his _____; from each according to his _____."

b. All evils in society are caused by _____.

c. If there was no private _____ people would have nothing to fight over.

d. Therefore, society should abolish private _____ and guarantee an equal _____ to every worker.

e. Each person must sacrifice his own _____ good to the _____ good of society.

23. Explain how Pierre Joseph Proudhon's ideas of government differed from socialism. *(pg. 307 – 308)*

_____

_____

_____

_____

24. Write the word that corresponds to each definition below: socialist, anarchist, egalitarian, capitalist *(pgs. 305 – 308)*

a. An _____ believes in removing all social, political, and economic inequalities among people.

b. A _____ believes that all productive property should be owned by the government, not individuals.

c. An _____ believes the government should not be able to force anyone to do anything.

25. *Answer the following. (pg. 308)*

a. What was Liberalism's answer to the "political question"? _____

_____

b. What was Liberalism's answer to the "economic question"? _____

_____

c. What was the "social question"? _____

_____

26. Write a word or phrase in each box to describe Antoine-Frédéric Ozanam. *(pgs. 308 – 309)*

27. Fill in the blanks to complete the ideas of Ozanam. *(pg. 309)*

a. Ozanam thought the economic systems of both socialism and capitalism were _____.

b. Because socialism gave the _____ complete power over citizens, it enslaved citizens to the _____.

c. Capitalism was just another form of _____ because it treated men as tools of _____
for the sake of the _____ and _____,

d. To save society from both socialist and capitalist oppression, the spirit of _____ had to triumph
over the spirit of _____,

e. Society should not be simply a great opportunity of _____ for the benefit of the _____.

f. Society should be dedicated to the _____ of all, especially to the protection of the _____.

g. Employers should not look on their employees as _____ but as _____ and fellow
_____ in the business enterprise.

h. Workers should receive a "_____ wage" – one large enough to support a worker and his family in
reasonable _____, as long as they lived _____.

i. A _____ should make enough money so that his _____ and _____ did not need to work.

28. Write **four** facts about Giovanni Mastai-Ferreti's life before he became Pope Pius IX. *(pgs. 310 – 311)*

29. Write **five** reasons why Pope Pius IX had the reputation of being a Liberal. *(pgs. 311 – 312)*

➢ _____

➢ _____

➢ _____

➢ _____

➢ _____

30. Why did Metternich and Pius IX's other critics object to the pope's attempts to reach out to Liberals? *(pg. 312)*

_____

_____

31. *Number the events in the order they happened. (pgs. 312 – 313)*

a. ____ Violent mobs gathered in the streets and demanded that the king dismiss Guizot.

b. ____ Throughout 1847, "Reform Banquets" held throughout France stirred up the people against the government.

c. ____ On February 23, soldiers fired into a crowd of insurgents, killing 50 people.

d. ____ Paris broke out into a full-scale revolution.

e. ____ On February 24, Louis Philippe abdicated and named his 9-year-old grandson, Count Philippe, as his heir.

f. _1_ Crop failures, unemployment, poverty, and lack of government reforms caused widespread dissatisfaction throughout France with King Louis Philippe's government.

g. ____ Crowds gathered in the streets of Paris, celebrating and singing "La Marseillaise."

h. ____ Fearing the Paris mobs, the deputies voted instead to end the monarchy and to establish a republic in its place.

i. ____ Liberals scheduled a Reform Banquet to take place in Paris on February 22, 1848.

j. ____ Louis Philippe and the royal family fled Paris, escaping to England.

k. ____ Prime Minister Francois Guizot banned the scheduled Reform Banquet.

l. ____ Hoping to appease the mob, Louis Philippe dismissed Guizot.

m. ____ Count Philippe's mother demanded that the Deputy of Chambers recognize her son as the king and appoint her as his regent.

32. *In each statement below* <u>cross out</u> *the ending phrase that would make the statement* <u>*false*</u>*. (pgs. 314 – 315)*

a. The revolution of 1848 differed from the first French Revolution in that …

    … it was not anti-Christian.
    … priests encouraged obedience to the new government.
    … there was no violence or bloodshed.
    … the king was not executed.

b. The revolution of 1848 differed from the July Revolution of 1830 in that…

    … it was less about political change.
    … the Liberals lost their power.
    … the revolutionaries were fighting more for social justice.
    … the workers were fighting against economic injustice.

c. The new provisional government of 1848 …

    … did not respect religion.
    … allowed all men in France to vote in elections.
    … was influenced by socialist ideas.
    … was a coalition of Liberals, Catholics, and socialists.

d. The workhouses established by the provisional government…

    … provided no real wealth-producing jobs.
    … paid higher wages than private employers did.
    … had a positive effect on the economy of France.
    … was supported by taxes paid by the bourgeoisie and peasant farmers.

e. The revolution in June 1848 was…

    … instigated by socialists unhappy with the new government.
    … begun after the government closed the National Workshops.
    … begun after the government ordered all able-bodied, unemployed workers to join the army.
    … a great victory for the socialists of France.

33. *Answer the following. (pgs. 316 – 317)*

a. What relation was Louis-Napoleon to Napoleon Bonaparte? _____

b. Why was Louis-Napoleon not living in France? _____

_____

c. What did Louis-Napoleon believe was his destiny?_____

_____

d. Why did the French bourgeoisie and peasants finally welcome Louis-Napoleon back to France?

_____

_____

e. What was the first position Louis-Napoleon was elected to in the Second Republic?

_____

f. Why do you think 5.5 million people voted for Louis-Napoleon even though they knew little about him?

_____

34. On December 20, 1848, Louis-Napoleon took the oath of office as the first president of France. *Fill in the blanks. (pg. 318)*

Speech bubble: *"I swear to remain _____ to the democratic Republic and to regard as _____ of the nation all those who may attempt by _____ means to change the form of the established _____."*

Thought bubble: How can I _____ the Republic and become _____ ?

Below is the Great Seal of France. The woman pictured is the Goddess of Liberty. (Does she remind you of a famous statue in the United States?) She is holding a fasces – a bundle of wood with a protruding axe blade. The fasces is the ancient Roman symbol of the authority of law. She is leaning on a ship's tiller, the lever used to steer a ship. The "S.U." on the vase stands for *Suffrage Universal* which means Universal Suffrage, the right to vote for all. "RÉPUBLIQUE FRANÇAISE, DÉMOCRATIQUE, UNE ET INDIVISIBLE" means "French Republic, democratic, one and indivisible." The date at the bottom is the date the Second Republic was established in France.

Name _____ Date _____

Chapter 12: **The Triumph of Liberalism**

1. Write **three** reasons why the Magyars of Hungary were discontent with Austrian rule. *(pg. 325)*

➢ _____

➢ _____

➢ _____

2. Write a fact about Lajos Kossuth and his political ideas in each box. *(pg. 325)*

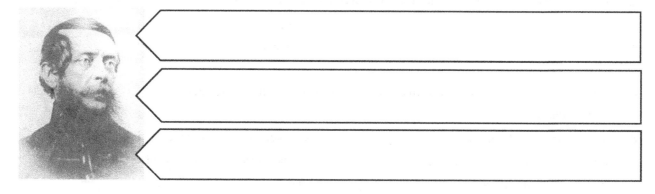

3. Number the events that led to Metternich's downfall in the order they happened. *(pgs. 325 – 327)*

a. _____ Meanwhile the violence spread to the suburbs of Vienna.

b. _____ On March 3, 1848, Kossuth delivered an address to the Hungarian diet, calling for reform not only in Hungary but in the entire Austrian Empire.

c. _____ A rumor spread through the crowd that the 12 had been arrested and troops had been summoned.

d. _____ Metternich thought the uprising was merely a street riot which he could handle by giving into one of the students' demands.

e. _____ The delegates admitted six students and six townsmen from the crowd into the *Landhaus.*

f. _1_ News of the Paris 1848 revolution reached Hungary and encouraged the Liberals.

g. _____ Metternich fled Austria to live as an exiled prince in London.

h. _____ Kossuth's address reached Vienna, where it stirred up excitement for reform.

i. _____ The crowd burst into the *Landhaus* and threatened the delegates until they agreed to send a deputation to the emperor.

j. _____ On March 13, an immense and angry crowd of university students and poor workingmen gathered outside the *Landhaus* in Vienna.

k. _____ The mob surged through the streets to Vienna's castle where Metternich was holding a meeting.

l. _____ Representatives of the crowd were admitted into the Council of State and demanded Metternich's resignation.

m. _____ After none of the ministers defended him or spoke in his favor, Metternich resigned.

4. List the **six** demands of the Vienna revolutionaries. *(pg. 327)*

➢ _____

➢ _____

➢ _____

➢ _____

➢ _____

➢ _____

5. *Fill in the blanks. (pgs. 327 – 328)*

a. Emperor Ferdinand I did not really rule the Austrian empire because he was _____-minded and subject to fits of _____.

b. The ministers of the _____ were the real rulers, but they were _____ without _____ to lead them.

c. The ministers began giving in to the revolutionary demands because they were afraid the _____ in Vienna would overthrow the _____.

d. The government established a National _____, entirely under the control of the _____.

e. The revolutionaries did not accept other measures suggested by the government and formed a _____ Committee to direct the city _____ of Vienna.

f. The Council of State was forced to _____ the committee and agreed to call a National _____ to draw up a _____ for the empire.

g. The delegates to the convention would be _____ by universal manhood suffrage.

h. _____ fled Vienna and called on all faithful Austrians to rise against the revolutionaries.

i. The angry Viennese revolutionaries forced the Council of State to give them control of the _____ and the _____ of the city.

j. The strong imperial army could not crush the rebels in Vienna because they were busy in _____.

6. *Using the map, follow the directions below. (pgs. 329 – 330)*

a. Draw a star on the capital of the Austrian Empire.

b. Circle the two cities in Italy that rebelled against the Austrian Empire in March 1848.

c. Who led the fight against Count Radetzky and the Austrians?

_____

d. Draw an X on the Italian region he was from.

e. Circle the Italian region that deposed its king and became an independent republic in 1848.

7. *Complete the following. (pgs. 330 -331)*

a. Circle the **three** Italian regions that were granted constitutions by their rulers in 1848.

Modena   Piedmont-Sardinia   Parma   Papal States   Tuscany   Lombardy   Sicily

b. Check the reforms that Pope Pius IX instituted in his government:

___ He increased the number of laymen in the government.

___ He established a representative government independent of the pope's control.

___ He created a two-house legislature with limited powers to pass laws.

___ He allowed the government to make laws about Church law and Church discipline.

___ He supported the revolutionaries' rebellion and sent papal troops to aid in the war against Austria.

___ He created an armed civilian force.

___ He granted a new constitution that established a secular state in the Papal realm.

c. Why weren't Liberals in Rome and the Papal states satisfied with Pius IX's reforms?

_____

_____

d. Why did the Italian Liberals finally turn against Pius IX? _____

_____

e. Write **four** reasons why the German people changed from peaceful to revolutionary:

➢ _____

➢ _____

➢ _____

➢ _____

8. *Number the events in the order the revolution in Germany happened. (pgs. 331 – 332)*

a. _____ A battle broke out between the Prussian soldiers and the townsmen in the streets of Berlin.

b. _____ On March 18, 1848, King Friedrich Wilhelm IV summoned a diet to consider to demands for reforms.

c. _____ The king and queen performed a public act of humiliation before the bodies of the dead insurgents.

d. _____ 230 revolutionaries were killed, but the army could not quell the uprising.

e. _____ News of Metternich's fall reached Berlin.

f. _____ Great crowds gathered in Berlin and demanded Liberal reforms.

g. _____ The king gave in to the people's demands and order his army to leave Berlin.

h. _____ Enthusiastic and happy crowds gathered at the castle to cheer.

i. _____ Fearing the crowds, the king ordered his troops to disperse the crowds.

j. _____ On March 21, King Friedrich Wilhelm pledged his support for a constitution and a national assembly.

9. What were the three colors of the German revolutionary flag? *(pg. 332)*

_____   _____   _____

10. *Fill in the blanks. (pgs. 332 – 333)*

a. In 1848, the German Confederation's *Bundestag* and Liberal politicians called for _____ to form a new national assembly.

b. The new assembly was called the _____.

c. It was made up of over _____ delegates who came mostly from the educated _____.

d. Few delegates represented _____ or _____.

e. The delegates could not decide whether Germany's government should be a constitutional _____ or a _____.

f. Nor could they decide what _____ should be included in Germany.

g. Both the Austrian _____ and the Prussian _____ were too busy dealing with _____ to control Liberals in Germany.

11. *Answer the following. (pgs. 333 – 334)*

a. Write **two** reasons why the peasants in Lombardy turned against the revolution.

➢ _____

_____

➢ _____

_____

b. Did Radetzky and the Austrians succeed or fail in their fight against the rebellion in Northern Italy?

_____

c. Explain why the revolutionaries in Vienna rejoiced at the failure of the Italian revolution.

_____

_____

d. What turned the Slavs against revolution? _____

_____

e. What weakened the cause of the Viennese revolutionaries? _____

f. Explain why the Austrian peasants lost interest in the revolution. _____

_____

_____

g. Give **two** reasons why violence broke out in Germany in September 1848.

➢ _____

_____

➢ _____

_____

12. *Number the events in the order they happened. (pg. 335)*

a. _1_   In August 1848, the government in Vienna announced that it would fire 20,000 public workers and cut workers' wages by 25 percent.

b. ____   Workers and students stormed the ministry of war in Vienna, while the city council took over the city government.

c. ____   On October 30, the imperial army drove back the Hungary army that had come to aid the defenders.

d. ____   A group of workers marched in protest against the government.

e. ____   Emperor Ferdinand called on his loyal subjects to rally to him.

f. ____   On October 23, 70,000 imperial forces laid siege to Vienna, which was defended by only 40,000 revolutionaries.

g. ____   On November 1, the imperial forces took Vienna, ending the revolution in Austria.

h. ____   National guardsmen and police clashed with the protestors, resulting the death of 25 workers and the wounding of 280 more.

i. ____   After their defeat in the "Battle of the Prater," the workers asked Hungary for help.

j. ____   Emperor Ferdinand and the imperial government fled from Vienna.

k. ____   Croatian leader, Josip Jelačić, marched his army to Vienna and joined the imperial army.

13. In each box write a fact about Count Pellegrino Rossi. *(pgs. 335 – 336)*

14. *Fill in the blanks. (pg. 336)*

a. _____ assassinated Count Rossi because he defended constitutional _____

and was able to prevent _____ in Rome.

b. After Rossi's murder, a _____ broke out against Pius IX and the _____ government.

c. Pius was forced to appoint a _____ ministry, but he refused to _____ because he said his

_____ power came from God.

d. Pius refused to put up any _____ against the Liberals because he did not want any useless

_____ shed on his behalf.

e. He took no part in the new _____ and forbade it to pass any _____ in his name.

f. With help, Pius escaped from Rome disguised as a common _____ and fled to _____ where he

was promised refuge.

g. Holding the very same _____ Pius VII had carried into exile, Pope Pius IX reassured his companions with the

words, "Be calm. God is with us. I carry the _____ on my person."

15. *Match the columns. (pgs. 336 – 337)*

A. Ferdinand I   [   ] Hungarian general who drove the Austrian forces out of Hungary

B. Franz Josef   [   ] ruling family of Prussia

C. Friedrich Wilhelm IV   [   ] first elected parliament of the German Confederacy

D. Lajos Kossuth   [   ] emperor of the Austrian Empire who abdicated

E. Artúr Görgei   [   ] powerful family who ruled the Austrian Empire for centuries

F. Hungarian Diet   [   ] first regent-president of the Republic of Hungary

G. Frankfurt Diet   [   ] King of Prussia who declined the crown of a united Germany

H. Habsburg   [   ] ruling body that declared Hungary independent from the Habsburgs

I. Hohenzollern   [   ] new Austrian emperor who wanted to unite all the Habsburg domains under one ruler and one parliament

16. *Answer the following. (pgs. 337 – 338)*

a. What were some of the nationalities that were part of Austria? _____

_____

b. Why did the Frankfurt Diet want Austria expelled from a united Germany? _____

_____

c. What was the greatest German state after Austria? _____

d. Who did the Frankfurt king Diet want to be king instead of a Habsburg? _____

e. Was the Frankfurt Diet successful in creating a united German independent of Austria? _____

f. What country helped Austria in its fight against the revolutionaries in Hungary? _____

g. Was Hungary successful in its attempt to free itself from Austrian rule? _____

17. *Complete the following. (pgs. 339 – 340)*

a. In 1849 Vittorio Emanuele II became the new king of …

　　　　Sicily　　　　Rome　　　　Piedmont　　　　Tuscany　　　　Lombardy

b. Which one of these men was a member of the Triumvirate of Rome?

　　　　Garibaldi　　　Mazzini　　　Duke Leopold II　　　Pius IX

c. Cross out the statements that do <u>not</u> describe the republican government of Rome.

It was inept and weak.
It was ruled by the Roman Diet.
It was truly democratic and had high ideals.
It was successful in bringing peace to Rome.
It could not protect its citizens from robberies, murders, and other crimes committed by private gangs.
It was not financial stable and was in constant need of money.
It respected the Church and was careful not to insult Catholic religious feelings.

d. Fill in the blanks to show how the Roman republican government treated the Church:

- It shot off _____ in the piazza of St. Peter's basilica on _____.

- It held a republican victory ceremony over _____ on Easter Sunday.

- It seized sacred _____ and destroyed works of _____.

- _____ were murdered.

- It declared all _____ government property and turned them into _____halls and _____.

e. Circle the nations that came to the pope's aid in 1849 to overthrow the revolution and restore him to power:

Piedmont-Sardinia   Spain   France   Russia   Hungary   Austria   Sicily

f. Rome's republican army was led by…

Giuseppe Garibaldi   Nicholas Oudinot   Louis Napoleon

g. Underline the accomplishments of the French forces in Rome:

It forced the republican government to surrender.
It captured Garibaldi and brought him back to Rome for trial.
It reestablished the pope's temporal rule in Rome.
It brought an end to the revolution.

h. Cross out the statements that do not explain why Pius IX did not immediately return to Rome:

The Roman cardinals elected a regent to rule in the pope's place.
Louis-Napoleon insisted that the pope establish a Liberal government.
Louis-Napoleon wanted the pope to make the Code Napoléon the law of the Papal States.
Louis-Napoleon was trying to control the pope.
The Redshirts were threatening to assassinate the pope.

i. Circle the Italian regions where the counterrevolutionaries were victorious in 1849:

Tuscany   Piedmont   Sicily   Papal States   Venice   Tangiers

18. Explain how Louis-Napoleon went from prince-president to Napoleon III, Emperor of France. *(pgs. 343-344)*

_____
_____
_____
_____
_____
_____
_____
_____
_____
_____

19. *Complete the following. (pgs. 344 – 345)*

a. Check the statements that correctly describe Napoleon III's government:

_____ The new Legislative Body of France was powerful and kept Napoleon under its control.

_____ The members of the Legislative Body were elected by universal suffrage.

_____ Political candidates who opposed Napoleon's policies could be charged with treason, imprisoned, or deported.

_____ An enormous government bureaucracy developed in Paris.

_____ It remained true to the republican goals of the 1848 revolution.

_____ A network of police was established to detect and arrest those planning sedition against the government.

b. Check the statements that correctly describe Napoleon III's political ideas:

_____ He believed in the divine right of kings.

_____ He believed he should unite all the French people and guide them toward justice.

_____ France should go to war with other nations to spread republican ideals.

_____ Socialist ideas of Saint-Simon could help France become prosperous.

_____ France and all Europe should become industrialized under the direction of scientific experts.

c. Check the reason Felice Orsini tried to assassinate Napoleon III in 1858:

_____ He was angry that the French bourgeoisie had lost so many political liberties.

_____ He wanted to take revenge on the French for humbling the Russians in the Crimean War.

_____ He believed that French troops in Rome were hindering attempts to unify Italy.

20. *Answer the following. (pgs. 345 – 346)*

a. How did Pius IX's attitude towards Liberals change when he returned to Rome?

_____

_____

b. What state in Italy had the only constitution after 1849? _____

c. What two jobs did the Count of Cavour hold in Victor Emanuele's government?

_____

d. Why did Cavour have the reputation of being a dangerous Liberal? _____

_____

_____

e. Why was Cavour not popular with the Church? _____

_____

_____

f. Why did Cavour increase the size and strengthen the Piedmontese army? _____

_____

g. Why did Cavour cultivate friendships with Great Britain and France? _____

_____

h. Why was Napoleon III hesitant to go to war against Austria? _____

_____

_____

21. How did Italy become one kingdom? *Fill in the blanks to complete the steps. (347 – 351)*

a. In July 1858, _____ made a secret agreement with Cavour to help Piedmont-Sardinia drive the Austrians from _____ and Venezia.

b. When the agreement was made public, Austria angrily demanded that Piedmont _____its large army.

c. When Cavour refused Austria's demand, Austria declared _____ on Piedmont-Sardinia.

d. By July 1859, the _____ and Piedmontese forces had driven the Austrians from _____.

e. Meanwhile, revolutionaries in central Italy had driven the Austrian-backed rulers from _____, _____, and _____ and had declared the independence of _____ from the Papal States.

f. When _____ learned of the revolutions in central Italy and that _____ might enter the war on Austria's side, he decided to break with Cavour and make _____ with Austria.

g. In July 1859, _____ and King _____ signed an armistice with Austria.

h. In the armistice, Piedmont-Sardinia gained _____ while Austria kept Venezia.

i. In early 1860, Cavour made a deal with _____ that allowed Piedmont-Sardinia to _____ central Italy, if the people there wanted it.

j. In March 1860, the people of Modena, _____, Tuscany, and _____ voted almost unanimously to join Piedmont-Sardinia.

k. In May 1860, with the support of Cavour and the British, Giuseppe Garibaldi led an invasion of _____.

l. Garibaldi's army conquered the island of _____ and then marched north where he conquered _____, the capital city.

m. Fearing Garibaldi would make himself dictator of _____, Cavour and King Vittorio Emanuele led a Piedmontese army south to _____.

n. On their way south, the Piedmontese battled the papal army and captured the papal lands of _____and the _____.

o. When the Piedmontese reached _____ in November 1860, Garibaldi agreed to _____ his forces to them.

p. The Kingdom of the two Sicilies voted to be _____ to Piedmont-Sardinia.

q. All of Italy, except for Venezia, _____, and the _____ now belonged to Piedmont-Sardinia.

r. In March 1861, _____ was proclaimed king of Italy.

s. For the first time since the _____ century, Italy was united under one king and government with one Liberal _____.

22. What were Cavour's words on his deathbed? *(pg. 352)*

23. *Answer the following. (pg. 352)*

a. Why did Napoleon III lose the support of French Catholics after his Italian adventure?

_____

_____

b. Why did Napoleon lose the support of the French Liberals? (Hint: Think about how the war of 1859 was ended.)

_____

_____

c. Did Napoleon's Italian adventure weaken or strengthen his dictatorship in France?

_____

d. Napoleon hoped that by weakening the power of Austria, France would become stronger. What happened instead?

_____

24. This chapter is called "The Triumph of Liberalism." In the space below, explain why.

Chapter 13: An Era of Change and Conflict

1. In each box write a fact about Karl Marx's early life in Prussia. *(pgs. 357 – 358)*

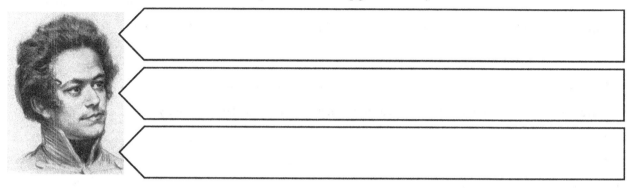

2. Write an important fact about Karl Marx's life in each of these cities: *(pgs. 358 – 359)*

Paris: _____

_____

Brussels: _____

_____

London: _____

_____

3. What were Marx's **two** most influential works? *(pgs. 357-358)*

_____   _____

4. Explain how the Industrial Revolution changed England in the 18th century. *(pg. 359)*

_____

_____

_____

_____

5. What additional changes came to England after 1830? *(pgs. 359 – 360)*

_____

_____

_____

_____

_____

_____

6. *Complete the following. (pgs. 360 – 361)*

a. Describe long-distance communication and travel before the mid-19th century.

_____

_____

b. Give two examples of revolutionary inventions made in communication in the 19th century:

➤ _____

➤ _____

c. Give two examples of improvements in transportation that occurred in the 19th century:

➤ _____

➤ _____

7. *Match the columns. (pgs. 357 – 361)*

A. proletarian   [   ] American who produced the first machine gun

B. pig iron   [   ] magnetism brought about by a current of electricity

C. industrialize   [   ] Frenchman who made the first true photography

D. electromagnetism   [   ] Englishman who established the first regular steamship service

E. daguerreotypes   [   ] someone who belongs to the working class

F. telegraph   [   ] Frenchman who perfected the process of making photographs

G. Henry Bessmer   [   ] American who invented a process for making sweetened condensed milk

H. Alfred Nobel   [   ] Englishmen who invented a better way of purifying pig iron to make steel

I. Richard Gatling   [   ] crude iron that is refined to make steel

J. Gail Borden   [   ] machine by which signals are sent long distances through electric wires

K. Samuel Morse   [   ] Swede who discovered how to make dynamite

L. Louis Daguerre   [   ] to turn over production to large factories

M. Joseph Niépce   [   ] photographic image made on metal

N. Samuel Cunard   [   ] American who invented the telegraph

8. Choose one of the inventions or inventors mentioned on pages 359 – 360 and do additional research. On a separate sheet of paper write a short report on your topic.

9. *Complete the following sentences. (pgs. 361 - 362)*

a. The most industrialized country in the world in the mid-19th century was _____.

b. This country followed the economic ideas of Liberal _____ capitalism.

c. These ideas were developed by the Englishmen _____ in his book _____ *of Nations.*

d. This economist said that _____ should not try to control economic activity by regulating _____ or _____ or placing any restrictions on business.

e. He thought that each person should be allowed to follow his own _____ in the creation of wealth for himself.

f. Economists in the _____ School said that employees should never demand higher _____ than their employers were willing to pay because it would go against the "laws of _____."

g. These economic ideas were favored by capitalists, _____, and even _____ which removed nearly every law that placed _____ on business.

h. Except for _____, most of the countries on the European continent were slow to industrialize and still remained mostly _____ land as of 1870.

10. Complete this chart of the social order before the Industrial Revolution: *(pg. 363)*

11. The chart below shows the new social classes created by the Industrial Revolution. Under each name, write what kind of people belonged in that class. *(pg. 363)*

> **The High Bourgeoisie**
>
> **The Petty Bourgeoisie**
>
> **The Proletariat**

12. Explain what the aristocracy and the high bourgeoisie had in common: *(pg. 364)*

_____

_____

_____

_____

13. Read the statements below. If the statement describes the aristocracy, write "**A**" on the line. If it describes the high bourgeoisie, write "**HB**" on the line. *(pgs. 364- 365)*

a. _____ They pretended not to care about money.

b. _____ They were despised because they did not come from old families.

c. _____ They gained their position in society by the power of money.

d. _____ They were considered lazy, wasteful, and immoral.

e. _____ They did not produce wealth or anything useful.

f. _____ They were proud of being hardworking, orderly, and thrifty.

g. _____ They thought that riches were a reward from God for virtuous living.

h. _____ They inherited their wealth.

i. _____ They often were on the edge of poverty and had to borrow money to save them from ruin.

j. _____ They thought poverty was a sign of immorality.

k. _____ Their children were usually raised by nurses and governesses.

l. _____ They thought any hardworking, moral man could become wealthy.

m. _____ Their life was family centered.

n. _____ They preferred sentimental art and literature with moral themes.

o. _____ They thought honor and pedigree was more important than comfort and success.

p. _____ They thought religion helped make one a useful member of society.

14. How was the businessmen's work life often in conflict with the moral ideals of their home life? *(pg. 365)*

_____

_____

_____

_____

_____

15. Cross out the statements that do <u>not</u> describe the Petty Bourgeoisie. *(pg. 365 – 366)*

a. They were exactly like the high bourgeoisie, but with less money.

b. They were ambitious to become part of the high bourgeoisie.

c. They were worried that they might lose their place in society and slip into the proletariat class.

d. They were worried that their work might be replaced by factories.

e. They were illiterate.

f. Many of their children received university educations so they could move up the social ladder.

g. They read cheap novels filled with outlandish adventures and shocking stories of the rich and famous.

h. Their favorite author was Charles Dickens.

i. They tried to improve the cultural tastes of the proletariat.

16. In what ways was the urban proletariat worse off than the poorest peasant in the country? *(pg. 366)*

_____

_____

_____

_____

17. Complete the descriptions of working conditions in 19th century factories. *(pgs. 366 – 367)*

a. Workers labored _____ to _____ hours a day, _____ days a week.

b. The wages were not sufficient to _____.

c. _____ and _____ also had to work in the factories, but for _____ wages.

d. The work of tending factory machines was mindless and _____.

e. The mid-19th factories were _____.

f. Since the factories were badly ventilated, workers breathed in _____ and they

had no relief from the _____ of the machines.

g. Since there were few breaks, workers became _____ and _____.

h. Workers lost limbs and even their lives because there were no _____.

i. Employers fired maimed workers with no _____.

j. Crippled workers were forced to live on _____ or _____.

k. Generally, employers felt no _____ toward their workers.

l. Workers often lost their jobs or had their wages cut because _____.

m. The new capitalist economy underwent frequent _____ _____.

18. Write **four** sentences to describe the typical living conditions of urban workers: *(pgs. 367 – 368)*

➢ _____

_____

➢ _____

_____

➢ _____

_____

➢ _____

Extra Credit

Imagine you are a worker in an English factory. Describe your work and life.

Research and write a report about the British politician and reformer Anthony Ashley Cooper, 7th Earl of Shaftesbury.

Read *A Christmas Carol* by Charles Dickens.

19. *Answer the following. (pgs. 368 – 369)*

a. What did most opponents of Economic Liberalism or *laissez-faire* capitalism think needed to happen to solve the serious problems workers faced?

_____

_____

b. Write **three** labor laws reformers were able to get passed by Parliament:

➢ _____

➢ _____

➢ _____

c. What arguments did opponents of reform use to defend child labor? _____

_____

_____

_____

d. Describe the purpose of most 19th century labor unions: _____

_____

_____

e. What is one method workers can use to put pressure on employers to give in to their demands?

_____

f. Why did some people conclude that to bring about justice, there needed to be a revolution in business and society?

_____

_____

_____

20. *Match the columns. You may need a dictionary for some of the words. (pgs. 366 – 370)*

A. bourgeoisie	[ ] utopian community founded by Robert Owen in Indiana
B. sentimental	[ ] someone who wants beneficial changes instead of complete destruction
C. solidarity	[ ] description of ideal societies where everything is perfect
D. compensation	[ ] association of workers formed to protect their rights
E. union	[ ] peaceful French socialist who thought people should do whatever they wanted
F. strike	[ ] peaceful socialist and factory owner
G. reformist	[ ] based on feelings or emotions rather than reason or thought
H. utopian	[ ] feeling of unity or mutual help
I. New Harmony	[ ] peaceful socialist who thought workers needed to take control of government
J. Francois Fourier	[ ] middle class
K. Robert Owen	[ ] payment made to a worker who is injured while working
L. Ferdinand Lassalle	[ ] refusal to work in order to force employers to agree to workers' demands

Name _____ Date _____

21. *Complete the following. (pgs. 369 – 370)*

a. Write **three** improvements Robert Owen made in New Lanark: *(pg. 369)*

➤ _____

➤ _____

➤ _____

b. When Owen could not convince Parliament to pass laws to better conditions for workers, what did he decide needed to be done? *Underline the correct answer.*

Emigrate to America

Change the environment in which people are raised.

Overthrow Parliament and elect socialist members.

c. Circle the phrases that describe Owenite communities.

Population of 1,000 – 1,500   People do whatever work they wanted

No marriage   Complete freedom without rules

No private property   Children over 3 raised in common apart from their parents

Primarily agricultural   Military training to overthrow the government

International   Communal living

d. Were utopian socialist communities a success or failure? _____

22. *Answer the following. (pg. 371)*

a. How did socialists like Marx and Bakunin differ from socialists like Owen, Fourier, and Lassalle?

_____

_____

b. Write an important fact about Mikhail Bakunin in each box.

c. What revolutionary socialist group were Marx and Bakunin members of?_____

d. On what did the peaceful socialist base their socialist ideas? _____

_____

e. How did Marx want to defend his socialist ideas?_____

_____

_____

23. Fill in the blanks to complete the basic ideas behind Karl Marx's Communism. *(pgs. 371 – 372)*

a. There is no _____ and no life after _____.

b. Man is a _____ creature without an immortal _____.

c. It does not matter if man is morally _____ on earth.

d. Man's only purpose in life is to produce _____ for his own use and the use of others.

e. Since men are more _____ if they work with others, they need to live in a _____.

f. Every society in history is divided between the _____ oppressor and the _____ oppressed.

g. The _____ invented moral codes, _____, and _____ to control the _____.

h. History is a continual class struggle between the _____ and the _____.

24. Number these steps in the stages of history according to Marx. *(pg. 372)*

a. _____ The proletariat will rise up and violently overthrow the bourgeoisie.

b. _____ In these towns, a new social class was created – the bourgeoisie.

c. _____ The bourgeoisie established industrialism and the capitalist order.

d. _____ All government will wither away.

e. __1__ When most Europeans were farmers, kings and feudal lords were powerful.

f. _____ A temporary proletariat government will stamp out resistance to Communism.

g. _____ When towns grew, trade and manufacturing grew.

h. _____ Finally, there will be anarchy where people will live in harmony, without government or religion.

i. _____ The bourgeoisie oppressed the proletariat.

j. _____ The bourgeoisie wanted more economic freedom and political power.

k. _____ The proletariat will establish a Communist society where there are no social classes.

l. _____ The bourgeoisie overthrew the feudal system in the French Revolution.

25. *Answer the following. (pgs. 372 – 373)*

a. What is the "dictatorship of the proletariat" according to Marx? _____

_____

b. Describe Marx's perfect society: _____

_____

_____

c. Explain the disagreement between Marx and Bakunin: _____

_____

_____

_____

d. What are socialists who are followers of Marx called? _____

e. What are socialists who are followers of Bakunin called? _____

26. Write an important fact about Wilhelm Emmanuel von Ketteler in each box. *(pgs. 374 – 375)*

27. Fill in the blanks to complete some of Kettler's ideas. *(pg. 375)*

a. The teachings of St. _____ on the nature of man, human society, and the _____ can direct us toward the right solutions to the _____ question.

b. All the evils of the world are caused by _____.

c. The evils of the time can be overcome by Christian _____ and recognizing the _____ of every person of every class.

d. Both the defenders of _____ and the socialists had fallen into dangerous errors.

e. The Church has the right to speak about _____ and _____ matters because they involved _____ and the Church is the guide to the moral life.

28. *Answer the following. (pg. 375 - 376)*

a. Explain the Church's teaching on private property: _____

_____

_____

b. Explain why Ketteler condemned *laissez-faire* capitalism: _____

_____

_____

_____

c. Besides spiritual solutions, what practical solutions did Ketteler offer for the problems of his day? (Write four.)

➢ _____

➢ _____

➢ _____

➢ _____

d. Why did Ketteler finally decide that government had to become involved in the struggle for justice?

_____

_____

_____

29. *Match the columns. (pgs. 376 – 377)*

A. Louis Pasteur   [   ] microorganisms that cause disease

B. Joseph Lister   [   ] one who studies the natural world

C. Charles Darwin   [   ] a fundamental change

D. germs   [   ] French scientist who discovered germ theory

E. naturalist   [   ] idea that everything can be explained only by material causes

F. mutation   [   ] English surgeon who discovered that surgical cleanliness reduced infections

G. materialism   [   ] process by which more complex species develop from less complex ones

H. evolution   [   ] English naturalist who developed the theory of natural selection to explain the origin of animal and plant species

30. Write four reasons the death rate was reduced throughout much of Europe in the late 19ᵗʰ century. *(pgs. 376 – 377)*

➢ _____

➢ _____

➢ _____

➢ _____

31. Explain Darwin's theory of natural selection in simple terms. *(pg. 377)*

_____

_____

_____

_____

_____

_____

_____

32. *Answer the following. (pgs. 377 – 378)*

a. What do materialist believe does not exist? _____

b. What Christian belief does Darwin contradict? _____

_____

c. Why did Protestants have problems with Darwinism? _____

_____

d. How did businessmen use Darwinism to justify *laissez-faire* practices? _____

_____

_____

_____

e. How did Darwinism effect religion and belief in God? _____

_____

_____

Name _____ Date _____

Chapter 14: New Powers, Old Battles

1. *In each statement below* <u>cross out</u> *the ending phrase that would make the statement* <u>*false*</u>. *(pgs. 384 - 385)*

a. Pope Pius IX and Vittorio Emanuele were enemies because…

> … Vittorio Emanuele wanted to conquer Rome and make it the capital of Italy.
> … Vittorio Emanuele was a Communist.
> … Vittorio Emanuele had unjustly conquered papal territory.
> … Vittorio Emanuele violated the freedom and independence of the Catholic Church.

b. Pope Pius IX was worried about…

> … his problems with Liberals in Italy.
> … the persecution of Catholics in Poland by Russia.
> … the presidential election in the United States.
> … the anti-Catholic laws passed by governments in Mexico and South America.

c. People thought Pope Pius IX was a Liberal because…

> … he had tried to institute some Liberal reforms in the Papal States.
> … he did not think that everything the Liberals proposed was wrong.
> … he did not support *laissez-faire* capitalism.

d. Pope Pius IX's friendly attitude towards Liberals changed because…

> … they had not chosen him as the king of Italy.
> … the Italian revolutionaries had driven him from Rome.
> … they wanted him to give in to their demands without compromises.
> … he realized they would always be hostile to the Catholic Church.

e. The *Syllabus of Errors* was extremely controversial because…

> … people thought the pope was being "medieval" or an enemy of progress.
> … Catholics thought it needlessly set the Church against the "modern world."
> … it condemned the treaty between Napoleon III and Vittorio Emanuele.
> … it condemned popular Liberal ideas like religious liberty.

f. Pius IX insisted on keeping his temporal power because…

> … he wanted to be rich and powerful.
> … it was needed to preserve the freedom of the Church.
> … it kept the papacy from being controlled by the state.
> … it was a gift of God's providence and no one had the right to take it away.

2. Explain what Pius IX meant when he condemned "progress" and "modern civilization." *(pg. 385)*

_____

_____

_____

_____

_____

3. *Match the columns. (pgs. 384 – 386)*

A. encyclical   [   ] group of French Imperial soldiers who remained in France to protect Rome

B. *Quanta Cura*   [   ] international volunteer force dedicated to protecting the temporal and spiritual power of the pope

C. *Syllabus of Errors*   [   ] Italian mercenary army led by Giuseppe Garibaldi

D. Papal Zouaves   [   ] Pope Pius IX's encyclical letter about the errors of the modern world

E. Legion of Antibes   [   ] official letter from the pope to the bishops and faithful of the Catholic Church

F. Redshirts   [   ] list of ideas condemned by the Church

4. *Number the events in the order they happened. (pgs. 386 – 389)*

a. _____ The French government forces Napoleon III to send 2,000 troops to Rome to aid the papal force.

b. _____ In September 1867, Garibaldi's forces invade the Papal States.

c. _____ On November 3, the papal troops fight the Redshirts at Mentana and force them to retreat to the castle there.

d. _____ In October, insurgents set off bombs in Rome, killing 27 Papal Zuoaves

e. _____ Vittorio Emanuel's army withdraws from the border.

f. __1_ In December 1866, Napoleon III removes the French troops protecting Rome.

g. _____ During the night, Garibaldi abandons his men and escapes across the border.

h. _____ The greatly outnumbered French legionaries battle with the Redshirts for 27 hours at Monte Rotondo.

i. _____ In June 1867, a celebration is held in Rome for the 18th centenary of the martyrdom of Saints Peter and Paul.

j. _____ Vittorio Emanuele sends 40,000 troops to the border of the Papal States but does nothing to stop Garibaldi.

k. _____ In the morning, the remaining Redshirts at Mentana surrender.

l. _____ The French retreat and the Redshirts plunder and destroy Monte Rotondo.

m. _____ After the hard fight at Monte Rotondo, Garibaldi waits several days before moving against Rome.

n. _____ General Kanzler gathers a papal army of 5,000 men and marches out of Rome to fight the Redshirts.

o. _____ The papal army encamps at Mentana and prepares for further battle in the morning.

p. _____ In December 1867, the French Legislative Body commands Napoleon III to send more troops to Rome to protect the papal kingdom.

5. Describe how the papal army and Pius IX treated the Redshirts after they surrendered: *(pg. 389)*

_____

_____

_____

_____

6. Fill in the blanks to complete what Pius IX said to the wounded Redshirts: *(pg. 389)*

Behold me, my friends! You see before you the '_____ of Italy,' of whom your general has spoken. What! All of you have taken up arms against me and you find only a _____."

7. *Circle the correct word or phrase in **bold** to complete the sentence. (pgs. 386 and 389 - 390)*

a. An [**infallible/ecumenical**] council is a gathering of bishops that represents the entire Church and can declare doctrines that all Christians are bound to accept.

b. Pius IX felt it was safe to hold a council in Rome because there were [**French/Italian**] troops protecting the city.

c. The council that opened on December 8, 1860 was called the [**Vatican Council/Council of Trent**].

d. The pope wanted the council to give a clear answer to the errors of [**science/modernism**].

e. On April 24, 1870, the council approved the dogmatic *Constitution on the [**Church of Christ/Catholic Faith**]* which affirmed the fundamental teachings of the Catholic Church and gave the Church's answer to rationalism, materialism, and [**science/atheism**].

f. The constitution declared that faith and reason [**are/are not**] contrary to one another and that the teachings of the Catholic Church [**are/are not**] opposed to science.

g. On July 18, 1870, the council approved the *Constitution on the [**Church of Christ/Catholic Faith**]* which defined papal [**impeccability/infallibility**] and proclaimed it a doctrine of the Church.

h. This doctrine means that when the pope speaks as the Successor of St. Peter on [**matters of faith and morals/ all religious matters**] he cannot be in error.

i. In the summer of 1870, [**France/Italy**] withdrew its army from Rome after [**Vittorio Emanuele/Napoleon III**] declared war on Prussia.

j. Pius IX did not think Rome would be safe without [**Italian/French**] protection, so the remaining work of the council was postponed.

8. Write two reasons why some Germans did not support German unification: *(pg. 391)*

➢ _____

   _____

➢ _____

   _____

9. *Complete the following. (pgs. 391 – 393)*

a. In each box, write a fact about Otto von Bismarck's early life.

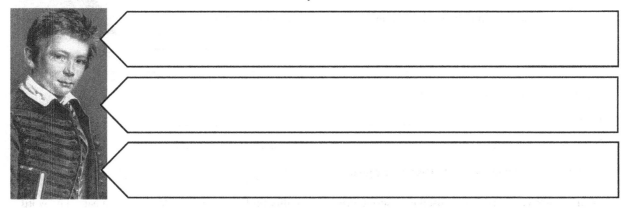

b. What did Bismarck think was the best form of government? *(Circle one.)*

   constitutional monarchy   parliamentary government   absolute monarchy   Liberal democracy

c. Fill in the blanks to complete the steps in Bismarck's political career:

When Bismarck was 32 he became a _____.

In 1851, he was sent as Prussia's _____ to the German Confederation's _____ at Frankfurt.

King Friedrich Wilhelm IV made Bismarck _____ to Russia and then _____.

In 1862, King Friedrich Wilhelm I made Bismarck _____ _____ of Prussia.

d. What was King Wilhelm I's great ambition for Prussia?_____

_____

e. What was King Wilhelm's trouble in achieving his goal? _____

_____

f. How did Bismarck solve King Wilhelm's problem and help the king achieve his goal?

_____

_____

_____

g. Write three of the repressive actions Bismarck engaged in as prime minister:

➢ _____

➢ _____

➢ _____

h. Fill in the blanks to complete this quote from Bismarck:

> "The great questions of the day are not to be decided by
> _____and majority resolutions... but by _____
> and _____!"

i. Thanks to Bismarck, what did Prussia's minister of war and chief of staff do?

_____

_____

j. What was Bismarck's great dream?

First, _____

Second, _____

k. What was the chief hindrance to Bismarck's goal? _____

Did you know? The word *Junker* used to describe Prussian nobility probably sounds odd to English ears. The word comes from the German word *jung* ("young") and *Herr* ("lord"). Thus, Bismarck was a young lord or nobleman – not a guy who collected useless stuff. Another interesting fact about the German language is that <u>all</u> nouns – whether proper or common - are capitalized.

10. Below are the steps that led to Prussia's war with Austria. *Number them the order they happened. (pgs. 393 – 394)*

a. _____ Bismarck made secret plans to annex both Holstein and Schleswig to Prussia.

b. _____ Bismarck ordered the mobilization of the Prussian army.

c. _____ Prussia and Austria went to war against Denmark.

d. _____ Bismarck declared Austria had broken the Treaty of Gastein and ordered the Prussian army to invade Holstein.

e. _1_ King Christian IX of Denmark annexed the German states of Schleswig and Holstein.

f. _____ Bismarck convinced Vittorio Emanuele of Italy to sign a secret alliance with Prussia.

g. _____ Bismarck pricked and annoyed Austria over Holstein and Schleswig.

h. _____ The war ended in August of 1865 with the Treaty of Gastein which temporarily placed Holstein under Austrian rule and Schleswig under Prussian rule.

i. _____ In November 1865, Bismarck convinced Napoleon III not to interfere in any war between Prussia and Austria.

j. _____ In June 1866, the diet of the German Confederacy ordered the mobilization of the federal army against Prussia.

k. _____ Austria threatened to ask the diet of the German Confederacy to send federal armies against Prussia if it would not abide by the Treaty of Gastein.

11. *Follow the directions below, using the map. (pgs. 394 and 395)*

a. Label the **Kingdom of Austria** and the **Kingdom of Prussia**.

b. Shade the areas that become part of Prussia after the Seven Week's War.

c. The darker line on the map shows the border of the German Confederation <u>before</u> the Seven Week's War.
Draw the new border of the Northern Confederation <u>after 1866</u>.

d. Who became president of the new Northern Confederation?

_____

e. Circle the regions that became part of the new Southern Confederation.

f. Draw an **X** on the region that was cut off from Germany after 1866.

g. Write "**Italy**" on the region that was given to Italy in the Treaty of Prague.

h. What country became the most powerful state in Germany after the Seven Year's War?

_____

12. *Complete the following. (pgs. 396 – 398)*

a. What did Napoleon III think was the best way to become popular with his army? *Underline the answer.*

Hold a plebiscite.　　　　Win a war.　　　　Reestablish the republic.　　　　Buy new uniforms.

b. Who became a hero because of the Seven Year's War? *Underline the answer.*

Napoleon III　　　Wilhelm I　　　Bismarck　　　Léon Gambetta

c. Why did the southern German states not want to unite with Prussia? *Check every true statement.*

___ They wanted to keep their local independence.
___ They thought Prussia's government was too oppressive.
___ They wanted to unite with the Austrian Empire.
___ They did not want to be ruled by a Protestant government.

d. What did Bismarck think would convince the southern German states to unite with Prussia? *Underline the answer.*

a war against France　　　a war against Austria　　　a new pro-Catholic political party

e. Why was there deep, anti-French feelings in Germany? *Underline the answer.*

Germany was jealous that France was the cultural center of the world.
Many Germans had been executed in the French Revolution.
France had interfered in Germany for centuries to keep it disunited and weak.

f. Explain what Bismarck did to trick Napoleon III into declaring war on Prussia in 1870.

_____

_____

_____

_____

_____

13. *Fill in the blanks. (pgs. 398 – 400)*

a. The _____ army was in a deplorable condition and not well prepared for war.

b. The _____ army was the most disciplined army in Europe.

c. The Franco-Prussian war was mostly fought in the region of _____.

d. The Prussian forces were commanded by General _____.

e. The French forces were commanded by Marshal _____ and _____.

f. Throughout August 1870, the _____ suffered defeat after defeat.

g. After the deadly Battle of Sedan, _____ surrendered his army and himself to the _____ on September 2.

h. When news of _____'s defeat and capture reached _____, mobs condemned the empire and republicans proclaimed _____ a republic.

i. The new government was called the Government of _____.

j. _____ offered an armistice to bring the war to an end, but the new republic rejected the terms and refused to surrender.

k. The _____ formed new armies to continue the fight, while the _____ began a siege of _____.

14. *Number the events in the order they happened. (pgs. 400 – 404)*

a. ____ Vittorio Emanuel sent 60,000 troops to invade the Papal States.

b. ____ Pius IX refused.

c. ____ The papal army bravely resisted the attack.

d. ____ On September 20, 1870, the Italian army began its bombardment of Rome.

e. ____ The outnumbered papal army fought the invaders, but eventually had to retreat to Rome.

f. ____ The Italians broke through the walls about 10:00 a.m. and Kanzler raised the white flag.

g. ____ Pope Pius IX condemned the annexation and refused to recognize the authority of the Italian government.

h. ____ When the Italian army entered the city, they committed acts of violence and brutality for two days.

i. __1__ Vittorio Emanuele asked the pope to disband the Papal Zouaves and replace them with royal Italian troops.

j. ____ In June 1871, Vittorio Emanuel and his government entered Rome and claimed it as the capital of Italy.

k. ____ The pope told General Kanzler to surrender once the Italian army had breached the walls of the city.

l. ____ The pope refused to leave Rome and remained a voluntary prisoner in the Vatican.

m. ____ Even though most of the people did not come out to vote, Vittorio Emanuel annexed the Papal States.

n. ____ On October 2, Vittorio Emanuel called a plebiscite to ask the people of the Papal States to vote on whether they wanted to be annexed to the kingdom of Italy.

15. *Answer the following. (pgs. 400 – 404)*

a. Why did Vittorio Emanuele decide it was finally safe to invade the Papal States?

_____

_____

b. What lie did Vittorio Emanuele tell his troops about why they were fighting?

_____

_____

c. What **two** laws did the Italian Parliament pass so the world would not think badly of the illegal seizure of Rome?

_____

_____

d. What unjust acts did the Italian government do after the conquest of Rome?

_____

_____

e. How did the Italian officials violate the pope's spiritual authority?

_____

f. How did Catholics around the world show their support for and devotion to the pope?

_____

_____

16. *Answer the following (pgs. 404 – 406)*

a. Describe how Prussia's siege of Paris affected the Parisians. _____

_____

_____

_____

b. How long did the siege of Paris last? _____

c. What happened on January 18, 1871 in the Hall of Mirrors at Versailles? _____

_____

d. What did the French National Assembly abolish and establish on March 1, 1871?

_____

e. What were Bismarck's humiliating terms for France in the Treaty of Frankfurt?

_____

_____

_____

f. Why was the Franco-Prussian war a great success for Bismarck? What did it help create?

_____

_____

17. Check the statements that correctly describe the new German Empire. *(pgs. 406 – 407)*

a. _____ It was ruled by a *Kaiser*.

b. _____ The 25 states that made up the empire lost all their independence.

c. _____ Government power was shared between the central power and the state governments.

d. _____ It had a two-house legislature.

e. _____ All the legislative representatives were appointed by the emperor.

f. _____ All Germans 18 years or older could vote.

g. _____ After the emperor, the chancellor had the most power in government.

h. _____ The legislature could remove the chancellor whenever it wished and appoint a new one.

i. _____ The emperor could veto measures passed by the legislature.

j. _____ Since the government was democratic, the emperor did not have much power

k. _____ It was less centralized than Bismarck wanted it to be.

18. Explain why Bismarck disliked Catholics. *(pgs. 407 – 408)*

_____

_____

_____

_____

19. *Match the columns. (406 – 409)*

A. *Kaiser*

B. federal

C. *Bundesrat*

D. *Reichstag*

E. Iron Chancellor

F. Center Party

G. National Liberal Party

H. Otto von Bismarck

I. Ludwig Windthorst

J. Old Catholics

K. State Catholics

L. *Deutsches Reich*

M. *Landtag*

N. *Kulturkampf*

O. May Laws

[　] lower house of the German legislature made up of representatives elected by the German people

[　] Catholics who would do whatever the government demanded of them

[　] "war for civilization" or "culture war"; the conflict between the Church and the German government from 1872 to 1886

[　] parliament of the state of Prussia

[　] Catholics who objected to papal infallibility

[　] German word for caesar or emperor

[　] anti-Catholic laws passed by Prussia in May, 1873

[　] upper house of the German legislature made up of representatives appointed by the 25 German states

[　] German Empire

[　] political group, made mostly of Catholics, who opposed liberalism and many of Bismarck's policies.

[　] Otto von Bismarck

[　] government where power is shared between a central power and state or territorial Governments

[　] anti-Catholic political group and Bismarck's chief allies in the German parliament

[　] first chancellor or prime minister of the German Empire

[　] intelligent and eloquent Catholic leader of the Center Party

20. *In each statement below <u>cross out</u> the ending phrase that would make the statement <u>false</u>. (pgs. 408 – 412)*

a. Bismarck banished the Jesuits from Germany because…

    … he thought they were the cause of all the anti-Liberal ideas in the Church.
    … he thought they were a menace to the German Empire.
    … he wanted to keep the Jesuits from influencing German bishops.
    … he thought they were the leaders of the Old Catholics.

b. The May Laws passed in 1873…

    … placed seminaries under state control.
    … allowed only government approved priests to serve in Prussia.
    … eliminated all religious instruction.
    … violated the Catholic Church's right to be free from government interference.

c. Other anti-Catholic laws passed in Prussia from 1874 to 1876 ordered…

    … the imprisonment of any Catholics who opposed the government.
    … the closing of all monasteries and banishment of religious from Prussian territory.
    … the confiscation of all Church property.
    … the imprisonment of any priest who criticized the government in his sermons.

d. In response to the May Laws, Catholic bishops in Prussia…

   … called on Catholics to peaceful resist the laws.

   … excommunicated Bismarck.

   … told Bismarck they would not cooperate with attempts to enforce the laws.

   … refused to pay fines.

e. As a result of the May Laws, …

   … the devotion of Catholics to the Church was weakened.

   … every Prussian bishop and hundreds of priests were either in exile or prison by 1877.

   … tens of thousands of Catholics were not able to receive the sacraments.

   … the Center Party grew stronger.

f. By 1878, Bismarck had decided that…

   … the Kulturkampf could not destroy the Catholic Church in Germany.

   … he no longer wanted to be allied with the Liberals and their economic ideas.

   … he needed the support of Catholics and the Center Party.

   … he should ally himself with the Social Democratic Workingman's Party.

g. Bismarck thought laws should be passed to improve the conditions of poor workers because…

   … it was the best way to fight socialists.

   … it was the kind and just thing to do.

   … the Social Democratic Workingman's Party was growing in membership.

h. Conditions for Catholics improved in Germany …

   … in 1880 when bishops were allowed to return to their sees.

   … in 1879 when Bismarck resigned as chancellor.

   … after Pius IX died in 1878.

   … as the May Laws were gradually rescinded between 1880 and 1886.

21. *Answer the following. (pg. 412)*

a. Who was the successor of Pope Pius IX? _____

b. How did the new pope's style of ruling the Church differ from that of Pius IX?

   _____

   _____

   _____

c. Explain how the courage of Pius IX helped German Catholics:

   _____

   _____

   _____

Chapter 15: **Into a New Century**

1. *Fill in the blanks. (pgs. 417 – 418)*

a. After the Germans withdrew from Paris, the citizens of Paris voted in a new government called the _____

and proclaimed the _____ of Paris from France.

b. The Paris government was controlled by Jacobins, _____, Marxist, and _____.

c. Their flag was not the revolutionary tricolor, but the red banner of the _____.

d. The French National Assembly sent the army to overthrow the Paris _____.

e. The week-long battle in the streets of Paris was called _____.

f. During this time, Catholic _____ and clergy were arrested and _____, including the

_____ of Paris, Georges Darboy.

g. When the Paris resistance was finally overcome, tens of thousands of Parisians were _____ and

thousands were _____ or _____ from France.

2. *Match the columns. (pgs. 418 – 420)*

A. Adolphe Thiers   [   ] upper house of the French legislature

B. First International   [   ] revolutionary Communist organization

C. Communards   [   ] lower house of the French legislature

D. Third Republic   [   ] first president of France's Third Republic

E. Legitimists   [   ] Communist members of the Paris Commune

F. Orleanists   [   ] eloquent republican who supported moderate policies and had great influence in the French government

G. Bonapartists   [   ] Legitimist who was elected president of France after Thiers resigned

H. Leon Gambetta   [   ] idea the churchmen should have an official place in influencing the government and the social life of a nation

I. Patrice de Mac-Mahon   [   ] monarchists who wanted a member of Napoleon's family to be king of France

J. Jules Grévy   [   ] monarchist who wanted a member of King Louis Philippe's family to be king

K. clericalism   [   ] two-house legislature established by the 11th constitution of France

L. National Assembly   [   ] French republican government founded during the Franco-Prussian War

M. Senate   [   ] republican who was elected president after Mac-Mahon resigned

N. Chamber of Deputies   [   ] monarchists who wanted a member of the Bourbon family to be king of France

3. *Answer the following. (pgs. 419 – 421)*

a. What group at first dominated the government of the Third Republic? _____

b. What group eventually gained control of the Third Republic? _____

c. Which group was anticlerical? _____

d. Which group did most Catholic churchmen support? _____

e. What was Thiers' great success during his presidency? _____

_____

f. Why did Thiers resign? _____

_____

g. Did the 11th constitution of France re-establish a monarchy? _____

h. Who chose the members of the French Senate? _____

i. Who chose the members of the Chamber of Deputies? _____

j. Who chose the president of France? _____

k. Who chose the prime minister and ministers? _____

l. Why did Mac-Mahon resign? _____

_____

m. Whose interests did the moderate republicans support? _____

n. Whose interests did the radical republicans support? _____

o. What legislation did the republicans propose in order to remove the Church from education?

_____

_____

p. What did the ministry do about religious orders? _____

_____

q. What laws about marriage were passed in the 1880s in France?

_____

4. *Complete the following. (pgs. 421 – 422)*

a. Write **five** factors that contributed to the phenomenal growth in German industry after 1870:

➤ _____

➤ _____

➤ _____

➤ _____

➤ _____

b. Describe how industrialization changed Germany. _____

_____

_____

c. Write four problems industrialization brought to Germany:

➤ _____

➤ _____

➤ _____

➤ _____

5. *Finish these sentences. (pgs. 422 – 423)*

a. The problems of industrialization caused German workers to join the

_____.

b. Bismarck got the *Reichstag* to pass anti-_____ laws.

c. The _____ and the _____

opposed these laws.

d. Despite these laws, the _____

continued to grow and even gained more seats in the _____.

e. In 1881, Bismarck decided to propose measures that would help the _____,

such as _____ insurance.

f. The _____ Party supported Bismarck's measures.

g. The *Reichstag* passed Bismarck's measures and Germany became the first nation in the world to provide social

_____ .

h. In 1887, Bismarck pushed through a law that limited _____

and made Sunday _____.

i. The law also set up government supervision of factories to make sure they were _____

j. The Social Democrats did not think Bismarck's laws gave full _____

k. Bismarck was unsuccessful in halting the growth of _____

6. *Complete the following. (pgs. 423 – 424)*

a. What did Bismarck do to help Germany develop into the foremost nation in Europe? *Check the correct answers.*

_____ He planned wars to conquer rival powers.
_____ He maintained a well-trained and well-equipped army of 400,000 men.
_____ He turned to diplomacy.
_____ He kept France from making alliances with the major powers.
_____ He stirred up trouble between Russia and Austria.
_____ He sought peaceful alliances with other nations.

b. The League of Three Emperors was an alliance of the leaders of what three countries? *Circle the three countries.*

Austria   Great Britain   France   Russia   Italy   Austria   Germany

c. What three countries formed the Triple Alliance of 1882? *Circle the three countries.*

Austria   Great Britain   France   Russia   Italy   Austria   Germany

d. By 1888, what goals had Bismarck achieved? *Check the correct answers.*

_____ He had isolated France.
_____ He was on good terms with most of the major European powers.
_____ He had made an alliance with France.
_____ He had brought peace to Germany.
_____ He had made the rest of Europe unstable.

7. Complete the following. *(pgs. 424 - 426)*

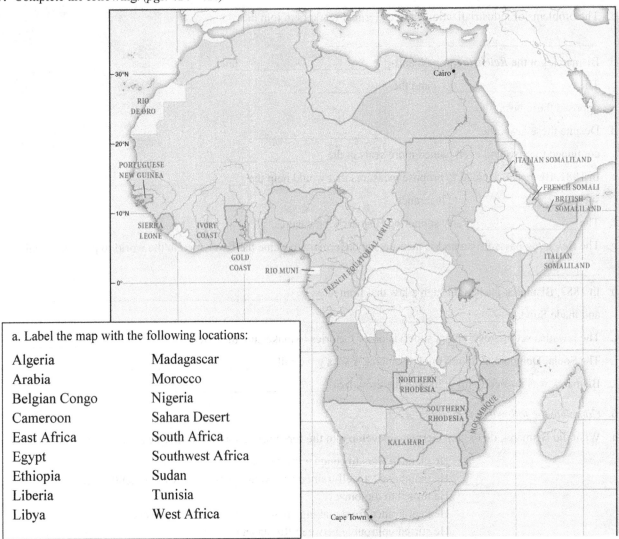

a. Label the map with the following locations:

Algeria	Madagascar
Arabia	Morocco
Belgian Congo	Nigeria
Cameroon	Sahara Desert
East Africa	South Africa
Egypt	Southwest Africa
Ethiopia	Sudan
Liberia	Tunisia
Libya	West Africa

b. List the seven European countries that colonized Africa: _____

_____

c. List the two countries in Africa that remained independent: _____

d. List four other places in the world that were colonized by European countries: _____

_____

e. Write two reasons European nations wanted colonies: _____

_____

_____

f. What groups in Germany were opposed to colonization? _____

_____

146

8. In each box, write a word or phrase that describes Kaiser Wilhelm II. *(pg. 426)*

9. *True or false? If the statement is false, change it to make it true. (pgs. 426 – 427)*

Example: *false* Kaiser Wilhelm II was Wilhem I's ~~son.~~
grandson

a. _____ Kaiser Wilhelm II wanted to be a the kind of king his grandfather had been.

b. _____ Kaiser Wilhelm did not oppose Bismarck's laws against socialists.

c. _____ Bismarck and the Kaiser disagreed about almost everything.

d. _____ Bismarck had been the real ruling power in the empire for 25 years.

e. _____ Kaiser Wilhelm I wanted to run the government himself.

f. _____ Bismarck forbade the other ministers to report directly to the kaiser.

g. _____ The kaiser ordered Bismarck to resign because he refused to obey him.

h. _____ Bismarck was happy to resign.

i. _____ The kaiser was sad to lose Bismark.

j. _____ An experienced chancellor and comptent ministers helped Kaiser Wilhem run the government.

k. _____ Kaiser Wilhelm renewed his treaty with Russia and followed Bismarck's foreign policy.

l. _____ In 1894, France formed an alliance with Germany.

m. _____ Wilhelm wanted to have good relations with Great Britain, but his policies brought them into conflict.

n. _____ Wilhelm interfered in Great Britain's war with the Boers in China.

o. _____ Great Britain was worried about Germany's expansion into China and the Middle East.

p. _____ Germany built up its navy so as to rival Great Britain's great navy.

q. _____ Great Britain formed an *Entente Cordiale* with her ancient enemy, Italy.

10. *Answer the following. (pgs. 428 – 429)*

a. Study the map on page 429. List all the colonies of the British Empire: _____

_____

_____

b. What were the sources of Great Britain's wealth? _____

_____

_____

c. Queen Victoria was merely the firgurehead of the British Empire. Explain why:

_____

_____

_____

11. *During Queen Victoria's reign, the major political parties in Great Britian were the* <u>Liberal Party</u> *and the* <u>Conservative Party</u>. *Read each phrase below and decide what party it describes. If it describes the Liberal Party write* **LP** *on the line. If it describes the Conservative Party, write* **CP**. *(pgs. 429 – 431)*

a. _____ Strong supporters of imperialism

b. _____ Aggressive towards other nations

c. _____ Wanted to give more British Citizens the right to vote

d. _____ Party of the artistocracy and old-fashioned landowners

e. _____ Party of the middle class

f. _____ Led by William Ewart Galdstone (G.O.M.)

g. _____ Led by Benjamin Disraeli

h. _____ Favored by Queen Victoria

i. _____ Favored free trade and opposed tarriffs

j. _____ Wanted to keep the Church of England as the state church

k. _____ Opposed establishing new British colonies in Asia and Africa

l. _____ Wanted a few men to own the vast majority of all the land in England, Scotland, Wales, and Ireland

m. _____ Former Tory party

n. _____ Wanted to keep peace with other nations rather than go to war

o. _____ Wanted to end the recognition of the Church of England as the official state church

p. _____ Opposed Home Rule for the Irish and wanted to keep the Irish poor and subject.

WILLIAM COX AND BENJAMIN BOX.

12. *Below are some of the accomplishments of Parliament between 1867 and 1881. If the action was done under Liberal control, write* **L**. *If it was done under Conservative control, write* **C**. *(pgs. 430 – 431)*

a. _____ Queen Victoria was given the title "Empress of India."

b. _____ Trade unions were made legal.

c. _____ Great Britian took control of the Transvaal Republic in South Africa.

d. _____ The suffrage was extended to more British citizens.

e. _____ A law to protect workers in factories and their rights was passed.

f. _____ Part ownership of Egypt's newly built Suez Canal was purchased.

g. _____ Transvaal was granted independence.

h. _____ A system of inexpensive, non-religious schools was created.

i. _____ Every man withing a city was given the right to vote for city officials.

j. _____ Catholics were allowed to attend the universities of Oxford and Cambridge.

k. _____ Laws to improve the housing and health of laborers were passed.

l. _____ Great Britain along with France took control of the government of Egypt.

m. _____ Almost every male in Great Britian was given the right to vote in elections for Parliament.

13. *Complete the sentences. (pgs. 431 – 432)*

a. The English had ruled over parts of Ireland since the _____.

b. Ireland was completely conquered by the English in the _____ century during the reign of Queen _____.

c. Land in Ireland was taken from the native Irish and given to _____

d. Catholics made up _____ percent of the population in Ireland.

e. Catholics in Ireland were forbidden to vote for _____

f. Catholics could not own land in Ireland, but had to work as _____ farmers on _____-owned estates.

g. No limits were placed on how much _____ a landlord could demand in Ireland.

h. If a landlord turned out a tenant, he did not have to _____ him for any _____
    the tenant made on the land.

i. The Catholic Irish had to support the established _____

j. Because the Catholics in Ireland were very poor, they often suffered from _____

14. *Complete the following. (pgs. 431 – 432)*

a. What right did the Catholic Irish obtain in 1829? _____

b. What political party did the Catholic Irish form? _____

c. Write **four** goals of this political party:

➢ _____

➢ _____

➢ _____

➢ _____

d. Put a check mark next to the goals <u>above</u> that the Irish were successful in obtaining.

e. What is Home Rule? _____

_____

15. *In each statement below <u>cross out</u> the ending phrase that would make the statement <u>false</u>. (pgs. 432 – 433)*

a. By the end of the 19th century, Great Britain consider Germany a threat because…

> … Queen Victoria belonged to the House of Hanover, a German family.
> … Germany had become Great Britain's chief industrial competitor.
> … Germany's navy was growing rapidly.
> … Germany was becoming more powerful in Africa and Asia.

b. Great Britain began seeking foreign alliances in the 1890's because…

> … Russia was moving into northern China.
> … The French were pushing into Sudan in Africa.
> … it felt threatened by Germany.
> … it thought isolation was better than foreign entanglements.

c. The British government made alliances with… *(three words are fasle)*

> … Russia.   … China.   … France.   … Germany.   ….. Japan.   … Austria.

16. Complete the graph below to show the economic state of British subjects in 1909. *(pg. 434) You will be drawing a line from left to right for each income group.*

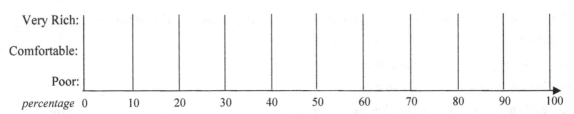

17. *Match the columns. (pgs. 433 – 435)*

A. Edward VII   [   ] new moderate Liberal party that allied itself with the Conservatives in Parliament

B. House of Hanover   [   ] king of Great Britain after his father died in 1910.

C. House of Windsor   [   ] Liberal member of Parliament who became Chancellor of the Exchequer

D. Liberal Unionist Party   [   ] dynasty to which Queen Victoria belonged

E. Labor Party   [   ] founder of the Liberal Unionist Party and influential member of Parliament

F. Herbert Asquith   [   ] Queen Victoria's son; king of Great Britain after her death

G. David Lloyd George   [   ] political party made up of socialists and representatives of trade unions

H. Joseph Chamberlain   [   ] leader of the Liberal party who became prime minister of England in 1908

I. George V   [   ] formerly called the House of Saxe-Coburg and Gotha; the dynasty to which Queen Victoria's husband belonged and the dynasty of the present rulers of Great Britain

18. *Answer the following. (pgs. 434 – 435)*

a. Explain the conditions in Great Britain that caused the Conservatives to lose the election of 1906.

_____

_____

_____

b. What party gained control of Parliament in the election of 1906?_____

c. What new party grew in influence after the election of 1906?_____

19. Fill in the blanks to show how the governing power of the British empire changed in 1911. *(pgs. 434 – 435)*

a. Parliament sought funding to build more _____ for the _____.

b. Lloyd George presented a budget in 1909 that placed new taxes on the lands and income of the _____

c. After debating the budget, the House of _____ passed the bill.

d. The House of _____ vetoed the budget bill.

e. Prime Minister Asquith dissolved _____ and called for new _____.

f. A coalition of Liberals, _____ Nationalists, and _____ Party members gained a majority in _____ in 1910.

g. The House of _____ passed Lloyd George's budget bill again and a bill that prevented the House of _____ from vetoing a bill passed by the House of _____.

h. The House of _____ vetoed both bills.

i. Prime Minister Asquith again dissolved _____ and called for new _____.

j. Liberals, Laborites, and _____ Nationalists again won a majority in _____.

k. The bill removing the House of _____ veto power was again passed by the House of _____.

l. The House of _____ again vetoed the bill.

m. Asquith told the House of _____ that the _____ would create new _____ who would support the bill if they did not give in.

n. The House of _____ backed down and approved the veto bill which stripped the _____ of their

power to stop _____.

20. *Match the columns. (pgs. 436 – 437)*

A. Tsar Liberator   [   ] grandson of Alexandr II; incompetent tsar

B. Aleksandr III   [   ] organized massacre of a people; genocide

C. Nikolai II   [   ] policy of forcing non-Russian people to adopt the Russian culture and language

D. *zemstvos*   [   ] Russian intellectuals who believed there was nothing they should not question

E. *dumas*   [   ] having to do with punishment for crimes

F. Nihilists   [   ] name given to Alexandr II after he abolished serfdom in Russia

G. *narodniki*   [   ] area in northern Russia with long, harsh winters where Russian prisoners are sent

H. Slavophile   [   ] elective governments in the rural areas of Russia

I. Russification   [   ] became tsar of Russia after his father was assassinated

J. pogrom   [   ] "men of the people" who tried to convince the peasants to become socialists

K. penal   [   ] elective governments in the cities of Russia

L. Siberia   [   ] someone who believes that the Slavic and Russian culture is superior to Western European culture

21. *In each statement below* cross out *the ending phrase that would make the statement* false. *(pgs. 436 – 437)*

a. A change that Tsar Aleksandr II brought to Russia was…

… establishing elective governments in the rural areas and cities.
… giving all Russian men the right to vote in local assemblies.
… court reform.
… permitting freer expressions of ideas.

b. More people became critical of Tsar Aleksandr II because…

… he wasted money and Russian lives in a war against the Ottoman Empire.
… he turned back many of his reforms.
… he planned to establish a constituational government in Russia.
… he carried out repressive measures against his opponents.

c. Aleksandr III thought the best way to fight anarchism and revolution was …

… to give in to some of his opponents' demands.
… with a strong autocractic government
… to impose Russian, culture, language, and religion on everyone in the Russian empire.
… to reestablish the old order of things in Russia.

22. *Complete the following. (pg. 437- 438)*

a. List some of the nationalities that made up 30% of the Russian empire: _____

_____

b. List the different religions in the Russian empire: _____

_____

c. Who helped the government carry out Russification? _____

d. Who had to report all "politically untrustworthy" persons to the police? _____

e. Describe the methods of Russification in the non-Russian areas such as the Baltic, Poland, Lithuania, and Ukraine:

_____

_____

_____

_____

_____

f. Describe how the Russian government treated the Jews: _____

_____

_____

_____

g. Write **four** other methods the Russian government used to fight opposition.

➢ _____

➢ _____

➢ _____

➢ _____

h. When he became tsar, how did Nikolai II respond to the plea for government reforms? *Fill in the blanks.*

"I intend to defend the principle of _____ as _____ as did my father."

i. How did the Russian economy change in the 1880s? _____

_____

j. Why did Russia want a Trans-Siberian railway? _____

_____

_____

23. *Number the events in the order they happened. (pgs. 438 – 440)*

a. _____ Since Japan wanted to move into Korea and Manchura, it did not welcome Russian troops in Manchuria.

b. _____ During the Russo-Japanese War, Russia was repeatedly defeated.

c. __1__ China allowed Russia to complete the Trans-Siberian Railway by constructing a line across Manchuria.

d. _____ Japan declared war on Russia on February 10, 1904.

e. _____ On September 5, 1905 the peace treaty was signed at Portsmouth, New Hampshire.

f. _____ During a Chinese rebellion in 1900, Russia moved troops into Manchuria to "protect" the its railway.

g. _____ U.S. President Theodore Roosevelt and Kaiser Wilhelm II negotiated a peace treaty between Russia and Japan.

h. _____ In 1903, Japan demanded that Russia remove all troops from Manchuria or allow Japan to move into Korea.

i. _____ Russia left Manchuria and gave Port Arthur, the connecting railroad, and half of Sakhalin Island to Japan.

j. _____ As Russia hesitated over Japan's offer, Japan launched a surprise attack on Russian warships at Port Arthur.

k. _____ The Russian troops remained in Manchuria after the rebellion was put down.

24. *Answer the following. (pgs. 441 – 442)*

a. Explain how Pope Leo XIII was different from Pius IX. Give examples of his actions that illustrate the difference.

_____

_____

_____

_____

_____

_____

_____

_____

b. What did Leo XIII reestablish in 1891 to show the world that the Church was not opposed to science?

_____

c. Many French Catholics were devoted to the French monarchy and opposed the Third Republic. Explain what problems that created.

_____

_____

_____

_____

d. What encyclical did Leo XIII write in 1892 to address those problems? _____

e. Write **three** main points of Leo XIII's encylical:

➢ _____

➢ _____

➢ _____

f. Write **four** new anti-Catholic measures the French government enacted between 1901 and 1905:

➢ _____

➢ _____

➢ _____

➢ _____

g. Write **four** benefits that arose from the French republic's attacks on the Church:

➢ _____

➢ _____

➢ _____

➢ _____

26. *Fill in the blanks. (pgs. 442 – 443)*

a. In 1891, Pope Leo XIII published the encyclical _____ which is the founding document of the Church's _____ teaching.

b. Leo XIII used the Church's traditional teachings on _____, _____ making, _____. and charity to answer the "_____ question" of the modern world.

c. In this encyclical, the pope condemned _____, but he also condemned the evils of *laissez-faire*

_____.

d. Some of Leo XIII's main points were:

➢ All human beings have a right to private _____.

➢ Society and the _____ should help as many as people as possible to own productive _____

➢ Workers have a _____ to be paid a wage large enough to _____ themselves and their families and _____ money if they live _____ . This is called a "just wage."

➢ Workers should not be treated like _____ or _____.

➢ Workers must not be _____ nor should _____ or _____ be forced to labor like men.

➢ Workers have the right to organize themselves into _____ and engage in peaceful _____.

➢ _____ should give in to the _____ demands of their workers.

➢ The production of _____ has a higher purpose than simply making men and nations _____

➢ People should use material goods to help them live a _____.

e. The encyclical inspired new Catholic _____ dedicated to _____ the social order and was even influential among _____.

f. Because of the moral dimension of economics, the Church has to be involved in solving social problems and if employers, workers, and governments _____ the Church, then …

"all human striving will be _____."

Chapter 16: Europe at War Again

1. In each cloud, write a word that describes what people thought the 20th century would be like: *(pg. 449)*

2. Write **six** reasons why there was so much optimism at the beginning of the 20th century. *(pgs. 449 – 450)*

➢ _____
_____

➢ _____
_____

➢ _____
_____

➢ _____
_____

➢ _____
_____

➢ _____
_____

3. Write **four** signs that showed all was not well in the world at the beginning of the 20th century. *(pgs. 450 – 451)*

• _____
• _____
• _____
• _____

4. Using a dictionary, write the definition for each of these words:

optimism _____

pessimism _____

progress _____

regress _____

5. In each box, write a fact about Father Georgy Apollonovich Gapon. *(pgs. 451)*

6. On the document below, write the petition that Fr. Gapon composed to present to Tsar Nikolai. *(pg. 451)*

7. Explain the situation in Russia that made the moment right for an uprising or conflagration. *(pg. 451)*

8. *Number the events in the order they happened. (pgs. 451 – 452)*

a. _____ Carrying icons and singing hymns, the workers processed peacefully through the streets.

b. _____ Fr. Gapon publically supported the strikers,

c. _____ The workers devotion turned to hatred and rage as several hundred were killed and thousands wounded.

d. _1_ In 1904, four workers at the Putilov arms and shipbuilding factory in St. Petersburg were fired.

e. _____ On January 9, 1905, a huge crowd gathered in the streets of St. Petersburg to process to the Winter Palace.

f. _____ One factory after another joined the striking Putilov workers.

g. _____ Fr. Gapon decided to organize the workers in a religious procession to present a petition to Tsar Nikolai.

h. _____ The workers at the Putilov plant went on strike in January 1905.

i. _____ As the procession approached the Winter Palace, the troops opened fire on the crowd.

j. _____ After learning of Gapon's plans, the tsar's ministers whisked the tsar out of the city and placed 12,000 armed troops throughout St. Petersburg.

9. In each box, write what happened as a consequence of Bloody Sunday: *(pg. 452)*

10. Explain the difference between the Liberals' and the Marxists' ideas to help the Russian peasants. *(pg. 453)*

_____

_____

_____

11. *Match the columns. (pgs. 453 – 454)*

A. Socialist Revolutionary Party   [   ] newspaper published by the Social Democrats

B. Social Democratic Party   [   ] faction of the Social Democrats that wanted violent revolution

C. Mensheviks   [   ] leader of the Bolsheviks

D. Bolsheviks   [   ] father of Russian Marxism

E. Iskra   [   ] Marxist group that tried to organize the peasants in the countryside

F. Georgy Plekhanov   [   ] Marxist group that tried to organize the proletariat of the cities

G. Vladimir Ilyich Lenin   [   ] faction of the Social Democrats that did not think Russia was ready for true socialism and supported working with Liberals to reform laws

12. Fill in the blanks to complete Lenin's ideas about revolution. *(pgs. 453 – 454)*

a. The _____ by themselves would never carry out a _____ revolution.

b. There needed to be an organization of professional _____ that would, like _____ carry the _____ of revolution to the _____.

c. The members of this organization needed to be highly _____, absolutely _____ to their leaders on the "Central Committee."

d. The members must be willing to _____ themselves and _____ for the revolution.

e. The members must allow nothing to _____.

f. The _____ of those who opposed the working-class revolution were of no _____.

13. *Complete the following. (pgs. 454 – 456)*

a. Write the **seven** reform promises made by Tsar Nikolai in his *October Manifesto* of 1905. *(pgs. 454 – 456)*

- _____
- _____
- _____
- _____
- _____
- _____
- _____

b. What reforms did Prime Minister Stolypin make to help the Russian peasants?

_____

_____

_____

c. Why didn't these reforms bring peace to Russia? _____

_____

_____

_____

_____

d. Complete this quote from Russia's Fundamental Laws:

"The All-Russian Emperor possesses _____ power. Not only _____ and conscience, but _____, commands _____ to his authority."

14. *Complete the following. (pgs. 456 – 458)*

a. <u>Circle</u> the various racial/ethnic groups that lived in the Austro-Hungarian Empire.

Bulgarian	German		Polish	Serbian
Croat	Greek		Prussian	Slovak
Czech	Italian		Romanian	Slovene
French	Magyar		Russian	Ukrainian

b. By the 20th century, the people of the Austro-Hungarian empire were "filled with the spirit of nationalism." What does this mean and why was it a serious problem?

_____

_____

_____

_____

_____

c. What did Emperor Franz Josef propose as the only way to break the power of the nationalists?

_____

_____

_____

d. Write the two changes that were made to the German constitution under Franz Josef's proposal:

• _____

• _____

15. *Fill in the blanks. (pgs. 458 – 460)*

a. In 1876, Austrian armies occupied the provinces of _____ and _____ on the Balkan Peninsula.

b. _____ nationalists claimed that these provinces rightly belonged to _____.

c. King Petar I of _____ wanted to unite all _____ under one kingdom.

d. _____ wanted to expand into the Balkans to gain control of the Bosporus.

e. _____ nationalists believed that all _____ nations should be united in some

way to _____ to form one great _____ and Orthodox empire.

f. In 1908, Austria-Hungary annexed _____ and _____ and announced that they were formally part of the empire of Austria.

g. _____ condemned the annexation and began mobilizing its _____.

h. Since Russia was _____'s ally and _____ was Austria-Hungary's ally, a war over the annexation could eventually spread across _____.

i. Fortunately, _____ backed down from war and accepted the annexation, but it harbored deep _____ against Austria-Hungary and did not abandon its hope for a great _____ empire in Eastern Europe.

16. *Underline the correct answer for each question. (pgs. 460 – 462)*

a. What African country did France want to take over?

   Algeria   Egypt   Morocco   Rio de Oro

b. Who ruled this country?

   Muslims   Italians   Africans   Spanish

c. What reason did France give to claim it had a right to establish a protectorate over this country?

   The lawless country bordered French Algeria.

   The weak country was being threatened by Germany.

d. Why did France need the permission of the other European powers to set up the protectorate?

   A protectorate violated the terms of the Triple Alliance.

   Europe had promised to respect this country's independence.

e. Which European countries gave permission and worked out diplomatic deals with France?

   Austria-Hungary   Great Britain   Spain   Germany   Italy

f. What three things did Germany learn from the Algeciras Conference?

   France had a strong friendship with Great Britain.

   Italy could not be relied on as an ally against France.

   The United States of America was Germany's only friend.

   Germany had become isolated in the world.

17. *Number the events in the order they happened. (pg. 462)*

a. ____ Germany sent an imperial warship to Morocco to protect its mining interests in the area.

b. ____ France refused to consider German's demands.

c. _1_ In October 1910, Moroccan tribes revolted against the sultan and besieged the capital city of Fez.

d. ____ Unwilling to go to war with Britain, Germany reduced its demands.

e. ____ The sultan, along with the foreign consuls in Fez, asked for help against the revolutionaries.

f. ____ France again rejected Germany's demands.

g. ____ France sent troops to Morocco, freed Fez, and occupied the city.

h. ____ Germany condemned the landing of French troops in Morocco as a violation of the Algeciras agreement.

i. ____ After many negotiations, France and Germany signed the Treaty of Berlin in November 1911.

j. ____ Eager to keep peace, France agreed to negotiate with Germany.

k. ____ Germany demanded compensation for the breaking of the agreement.

l. ____ The Prime Minister of Great Britain made it clear that his country would stand with France against Germany.

18. Write **three** ways the Second Moroccan Crisis affected Europe: *(pg. 463)*

- _____
- _____
- _____

Name _____ Date _____

19. *In each statement below* <u>cross out</u> *the ending phrase that would make the statement* <u>*false*</u>. *(pgs. 463 – 466)*

a. *Italia irredenta* or "unredeemed Italy" was …

>… the area where Italians lived but was not yet part of Italy.
>… the area formerly belonging to Italy, but now under the control of the Ottoman Turks.
>… land under Austrian rule that Italy wanted.
>… a name invented by Italian nationalists.

b. Italy went to war with the Ottoman Empire in 1911 because…

>… the Ottoman sultan had annexed Bosnia and Herzegovina.
>… it wanted more colonies in Africa.
>… the Ottoman sultan would not allow Italy to occupy Tripoli and Cyrenaica.
>… Italian nationalists wanted more land to create an Italian empire.

c. The Italo-Turkish war…

>… lasted about one year.
>… ended with the Treaty of Lausanne
>… made Libya an Italian colony.
>… was a victory for the Ottoman Empire.

d. The four countries that formed the Balkan League were…*(cross out the two incorrect names)*

>Bulgaria   Serbia   Herzegovina   Greece   Albania   Montenegro

e. The Balkan League declared war on the Ottomans because…

>… they were inspired by nationalism.
>… the Italians showed them that the Ottomans were not as powerful as they seemed.
>… the pope called a crusade to drive the Turkish Muslims from European Turkey.
>… they wanted the lands of Thrace, Macedonia, and Albania.

f. The Balkan War…

>… lasted seven months.
>… ended with the capture of Constantinople.
>… resulted in independence for Albania.
>… gave each country of the Balkan Leauge more land.

g. The Treaty of Bucharest…

>… brought lasting peace to the Balkan Peninsula.
>… settled the boundaries of Montenegro, Serbia, Romania, Bulgaria, and Greece.
>… ended the war between Bulgaria and the other Balkan countries.
>… did not completely satisfy any of the Balkan kingdoms.

h. The Black Hand of Serbia…

>… was a powerful terrorist organization.
>… carried out sabotage, assassinations, and guerilla operations.
>… was a way to help Serbia form a greater Yugoslav kingdom.
>… was condemned by the Serbian government.

20. Explain what it means to describe the Balkans as a "powder keg"?

_____

_____

_____

21. In each box write an important fact about each man. *(pgs. 466 – 467)*

Franz Josef

Franz Ferdinand

Karl von Habsburg

22. *Fill in the blanks. (pgs. 466 – 468)*

a. Since Franz Josef's only son was dead, the next in line to the throne was the emperor's _____, Archduke Franz Ferdinand von Österreich-Este.

b. Archduke Franz Ferdinand married _____, a Czech noblewoman.

c. Franz Ferdinand's children could not inherit the throne because his wife was not _____

d. The next in line to the throne after Franz Ferdinand was his _____, Archduke Karl von Habsburg.

e. Archduke Karl married _____.

f. Franz Josef apppoved of Karl's wife because she was _____

g. Serbian nationalists did not want Franz Ferdinand to become emperor because he planned to grant the _____ equal status with the Austrians and the _____ in the empire, which might upset Serbian plans to form a Yugoslav _____ separate from Austria.

h. The _____ formed a plot to assassinate Franz Ferdinand while he was visiting _____.

23. On a separate sheet of paper, retell in your own words the story of the assassination of Archduke Franz Ferdinand on June 28, 1914.

24. *Follow the directions, using the map below. (pgs. 469 – 472)*

a. Label: **Austria-Hungary, Serbia, Germany, Russia, France, Great Britain, Italy, Spain, Turkey, Belgium**

b. Color Serbia and it's allies one color. What was this side called? _____

c. Color Austria-Hungary and it's allies another color. What was this side called? _____

25. Complete this timeline by writing underneath the line and next to the date what happened on that day. *(pgs. 470 – 476)*

June 28, 1914 | July 28, 1914 | July 29, 1914 | August 1, 1914 | August 3, 1914 | August 4, 1914 | August 7, 1914 | August 23, 1914 | August 26 - 30, 1914 | Sept. 6 - 12, 1914 | Oct. 9, 1914 | Oct. 11, 1914

26. *Answer the following. (pgs. 473 – 476)*

a. What was the importance of the Battle of Tannenburg? _____

_____

_____

b. What was the Western Front of the war? _____

_____

c. What was the Eastern Front of the war? _____

_____

d. How many troops were gathered at the Western Front for the Battle of the Marne? _____

e. Who claimed victory in the Battle of the Marne? _____

f. What did General Erich von Falkenhayn think had to be done to win a modern war?

_____

_____

g. How did the German army put Falkenhayn's ideas into action? _____

_____

_____

h. What had the Germans accomplished in the war by the end of 1914? _____

_____

_____

_____

i. What had the Allied Powers accomplished by the end of 1914? _____

_____

_____

_____

j. How many German, French, Belgian, and British troops were killed or wounded in the first four months of the war?

_____

k. What are the two names given to this war? _____

27. In each shape, write a word or phrase used in the textbook to describe the war.

Chapter 17: The Great War

1. *Complete these quotes:*

"I bless _____, not _____."

Pope St. Pius X

The aim of my reign is "to strive in every possible way that the _____ of _____ should once more rule _____ amongst _____."

Pope Benedict XV

2. Explain why people said that Pope Pius X "died of a broken heart." *(pg. 481)*

_____

_____

_____

_____

3. *Answer the following. (pgs. 482 – 484)*

a. In the encyclical *Ad Beatissimi Apostolorum*, what did Benedict XV claim were the causes of the Great War?

_____

_____

_____

_____

b. What did Benedict XV think was the solution? _____

_____

_____

c. What did Benedict XV say about the pope taking sides in the war? *(Finish the quote.)*

"The Roman Pontiff, as the Vicar of Jesus Christ, who died for men, one and all, must _____.
And as the Father of all Catholics he has among the belligerents a great number of his children for whose _____ he must be _____ and without _____ solicitous. [I will condemn] openly every _____ by _____ side it may have been committed."

d. What was probably the chief reason the warring powers ignored the pope? _____

_____

_____

e. Explain the secret treaty between the Entente (France, Great Britain, and Russia) and Italy:

What did the Allies agree to do? _____

_____

_____

What did Italy demand in the treaty? _____

_____

f. With Italy's entrance into the war, how many fronts were the Central Powers fighting? _____

g. In each box, write a word or phrase the Benedict XV used to describe the war:

4. *Answer the following. (pgs. 484 – 485)*

a. Describe trench warfare on the Western Front:

_____

_____

_____

_____

_____

_____

b. Describe life in the trenches:

An aerial photograph of opposing trenches and No Man's Land

_____

_____

_____

_____

c. Describe the kind of chemicals used as weapons in World War I:

_____

_____

_____

_____

_____

5. Circle the names of **six** countries (or parts of countries) the Central Powers conquered between February 1915 and February 1916 in the war on the Eastern Front. *(pg. 486)*

Poland   Russia   Serbia   Albania   France   Montenegro   Lithuania   Latvia

6. *Match the columns. You may need a dictionary. (pgs. 486 – 487)*

A. contraband   [   ] not supporting either side in a war

B. blockade   [   ] exploration of an enemy's territory to gain information

C. belligerents   [   ] persons not in the military

D. neutral   [   ] airship or dirigible

E. indiscriminate warfare [   ] persons not engaged in fighting in a war

F. U-boat   [   ] goods that may not be imported, exported, or possessed

G. zeppelin   [   ] not making distinctions between military and civilian targets

H. reconnaissance   [   ] preventing goods or people from entering or leaving

I. civilians   [   ] undersea boat; German submarine

J. noncombatants   [   ] nations or persons who engage in fighting

7. *Fill in the blanks. (pgs. 486 - 487)*

a. The purpose of the _____ blockade was to stop munitions, arms, raw materials, and other necessary items from reaching the German _____.

b. The blockade gradually kept even _____ shipments from reaching Germany.

c. Because Germany had become industrialized, the blockade threatened to _____ not only the German army, but German _____ as well.

d. In response, the German navy laid _____ off the coast of _____ and Ireland.

e. Germany also declared unrestricted _____ warfare on _____ merchant ships.

f. On May 7, 1915, the Germans sank the _____, a ship carrying _____ passengers and a secret cargo of _____-manufactured munitions.

8. Draw an illustration of a zeppelin <u>and</u> explain what its use in war was. *(pgs. 488 – 489)*

9. In what way did the Great War depart from the code of ethics that had governed warfare in Europe for hundreds of years? *(pg. 489)*

_____

_____

10. Write the name of **two** battles that occurred at the Western Front in 1916 and describe their outcome. *(pg. 489)*

_____

_____

_____

_____

_____

_____

11. *Answer the following. (pgs. 490 – 492)*

a. Who were the Austro-Hungarian forces fighting on the Isonzo Front? _____

b. Were they successful in pushing the Austrians from the Isonzo Front? _____

c. Who were the Austro-Hungarian forces fighting on the Eastern Front? _____

d. Were they successful in defending the Eastern line? _____

e. What country joined the Allies in August 1916? _____

f. Half of what country fell under German control by January 1917? _____

g. Why was this conquest important to the Central Powers? *(Write two reasons.)*

_____

_____

_____

h. Who offered to mediate peace talks between the warring European powers? _____

i. Why was Kaiser Wilhelm willing to discuss terms of peace by late 1916? _____

_____

j. What four demands did the Allies have for peace?

_____

_____

_____

_____

k. Which demand would the Central Powers not accept?

_____

_____

_____

12. *In each statement below* <u>cross out</u> *the ending phrase that would make the statement* <u>*false*</u>. *(pg. 492 – 496)*

a. When Archduke Karl von Habsburg became emperor of Austria in 1916, his goals were to…

    … relieve the misery the war had inflicted on his people.
    … reform the empire's government.
    … take back lands that had been lost to the Allies.
    … end the war.

b. Karl I reformed the conduct of his own army by…

    … having political prisoners flogged instead of hung.
    … ending strategic bombing raids.
    … strictly limiting the use of poison gas.

c. Emperor Karl did not turn the Dual Monarchy into a federation of autonomous states because…

    … the powerful Magyar landowners in Hungary were opposed to it.
    … he was afraid his empire would become smaller.
    … the German members of the *Reichsrat* were opposed to it.
    … his ministers would not support his policy in the *Reichsrat*.

d. Emperor Karl's attempts to bring peace to Europe were unsuccessful because…

    … his ministers and the German high command were opposed to his peace efforts.
    … his wife's brothers undermined his peace proposals.
    … the Allies believed that Germany was weakening and they would soon win the war.
    … the Allies had secretly promised to obtain Austrian territories for Italy.

e. The United States initially kept out of the war in Europe, but…

    … President Wilson publicly spoke out against the Central Powers.
    … loaned the Allies $3.5 billion.
    … sent guns, ammunition, and artillery to the Allied armies.

f. Relations between the United States and the Central Powers became worse after…

    … Germany resumed unrestricted submarine warfare.
    … German ambassadors set off bombs in American munition factories.
    … a U-boat sank the British *Laconia*, killing eight American citizens on board.
    … the U.S. discovered that Germany was trying to make an alliance with Mexico.

g. After the U.S. Congress declared war on Germany on April 6, 1917…

    … it loaned the Allied governments $7 billion.
    … began a massive shipbuilding project.
    … instituted a draft of U.S. men ages 21 to 30.
    … immediately sent 625,000 troops to Europe.

13. Complete President Woodrow Wilson's reason for U.S. involvement in the Great War: *(pg. 496)*

"The world must be made _____ for _____."

14. *Circle the word or phrase in bold that correctly completes each sentence. (pgs. 497 – 498)*

a. In 1917, German U-boat warfare caused severe food shortages in **[Great Britain/the United Sates]**.

b. U.S. warships **[were insignificant in reducing/dramatically reduced]** the number of ships sunk by U-boats.

c. Allied campaigns along the Western Front in 1917 **[did/did not]** significantly change the situation there.

d. During the 1917 fighting on the Western Front, the **[Allies/Germans]** suffered more casualties.

e. The Allies were **[more/less]** successful on the Eastern Front.

f. In July 1917, Greece entered the war on the side of the **[Central Powers/Allies]**.

15. In each box write a word or phrase to describe Rasputin. *(pg. 498)*

16. *Answer the following. (pgs. 498 – 499)*

a. Explain how Rasputin gained control over the royal family of Russia.

Tsarevich Alexi

b. What were the negative effects of Rasputin's influence?

c. Describe conditions in Russia during World War I:

d. What happened to Rasputin?

170

17. *Number the Russian events of 1917 in the order they happened. (pg. 500)*

a. _____ The socialists established their own executive committee to govern Petrograd.

b. _____ The police opened fire on rioters, killing nine people.

c. _____ The revolutionaries rejected the tsar's concessions and demanded his abdication.

d. __1__ On March 8, female factory workers in Petrograd started shouting "Bread for the workers!" in the streets.

e. _____ Tsar Nikolai sent an army to Petrograd to end the revolution.

f. _____ Seven days later, the new government arrested Nikolai and his family, imprisoning them in the imperial palace.

g. _____ Workers from all over the city joined the protest and grew violent.

h. _____ Tsar Nikolai decided to give in to the demands of the Liberal revolutionaries and promised reforms.

i. _____ During the crisis, the Russian Parliament established a Liberal government in Petrograd.

j. _____ Three days later, workers again gathered in the streets.

k. _____ Soldiers began joining the protestors and socialist revolutionaries began organizing.

l. _____ The Duma admitted two socialist representatives into the parliament and took control of the revolution.

m. _____ When the troops reached the city, they joined the rebellion.

n. _____ Seeing that he had no choice, Nikolai reluctantly gave up the throne on March 15th.

18. Complete Vladimir Lenin's criticism of Russia's new revolutionary government: *(pg. 501)*

"The people need _____. The people need _____ and _____, and they give you _____, _____, no _____, and the _____ remains with the landowners."

19. Read each statement below and decide whether it describes the Liberal government of Russia or the government the socialists wanted. *Write **L** or **S** on the line. (pg. 501)*

a. _____ Recognized as a legitimate by the U.S., Great Britain, France, and Italy.

b. _____ Great estates should be seized without compensation to their owners and turned over to the peasants.

c. _____ Russia should withdraw from the war and make peace with the Central Powers.

d. _____ It represents the middle class, industrialists, and constitutionalists.

e. _____ It represents the peasants, workers, and soldiers.

f. _____ A new constitution and a few reforms are all Russia needs.

g. _____ Russia should remain involved in the war with the Allies.

h. _____ Factories should be taken from the capitalists and turned over to the workers.

20. What was Lenin's criticism of his fellow socialists? *(pg. 501)*

_____

_____

21. *Match the columns. (pgs. 501 – 502)*

A. Lenin   [   ] prime minister of Russia's provisional government

B. Stalin   [   ] moderate socialist party

C. Trotsky   [   ] radical socialist party led by Lenin

D. Kerensky   [   ] former Menshevik who joined the Bolsheviks and became Lenin's second in command

E. Bolsheviks   [   ] Russian word meaning "council"

F. Mensheviks   [   ] radical and relentless socialist, who some thought was a madman

G. soviet   [   ] Bolshevik who thought the socialists should cooperate with the Liberal government

22. Fill in the blanks to complete the seven points of Pope Benedict XV's peace plan: *(pg. 503)*

a. Relations between nations should be governed by _____ rather than the "material force of arms" - _____

b. Nations must reduce their _____ .

c. Instead of relying on _____ and _____ to settle disputes, nations should establish an _____ institution with the ability to settle international _____ and the power to _____ its decrees.

d. All nations should enjoy "true liberty and common rights over the _____ ."

e. The warring nations should seek no _____ from each other for the _____ and _____ of the war. "To continue such carnage only for _____ reasons would be inconceivable."

f. Each side should _____ foreign territories occupied during the war. Germany should evacuate _____ and _____ , and in return, the Allies should restore to _____ her foreign _____ .

g. Where different nations _____ the same territory, they should discuss the future of the disputed territory in the light of _____ . They especially should consider what the _____ of the territory desire as well as the "general _____ " of all nations.

23. Circle the points <u>above</u> that were similar to Germany's proposed four peace points. *(pg. 502)*

24. Circle the names of the countries that supported Benedict's peace proposal. *(pg. 503)*

Austria   Great Britain   United States   Germany   Italy   France   Bulgaria   Ottoman Empire

25. Why do you think the Pope Benedict's efforts to bring peace failed?

_____

_____

_____

_____

_____

Did you know? Besides trying to bring about peace, Pope Benedict XV worked tirelessly to alleviate the sufferings of all peoples during the war. He helped negotiate exchanges of prisoners and promises to improve the conditions of prisoners. Benedict nearly bankrupted the Vatican, sending money to the desperate and starving. He was especially concerned about the fate of children in war-torn countries. He encouraged the children of wealthier countries to contribute to the *Save the Children* fund that he established to help the suffering children in Central Europe.

26. Give **three** signs of chaos in Russia in 1917: *(pg. 504)*

- _____
- _____
- _____

27. *Number the events in the order they happened. (pgs. 504 – 505)*

a. _____ In October, Lenin arrived in Petrograd and convinced the Bolsheviks to stage an armed uprising.

b. _1_ In July 1917, Aleksandr Kerensky organized a new provisional government for Russia.

c. _____ The Bolsheviks arrested the members of Kerensky's government and proclaimed a new government.

d. _____ The Bolsheviks accused Kerensky of being against democratic government.

e. _____ In September, Trotsky was released from prison and became chairman of the Petrograd Soviet.

f. _____ General Kornilov ordered his troops to march to Petrograd to overthrow Kerensky's government.

g. _____ Kornilov surrendered to Kerensky and was imprisoned.

h. _____ Railroad workers stopped Kornilov by tearing up the tracks leading into Petrograd.

i. _____ Kerensky postponed elections from September 30 to November 25.

j. _____ More workers joined the Bolshevik party and the Bolsheviks gained control of the Petrograd Soviet.

k. _____ On the night of November 6, armed Bolsheviks captured the bridges spanning the Neva River, seized railroad stations, telegraph and telephone offices, power plants, and the Bank of Russia.

28. *Fill in the blanks. (pgs. 505 – 506)*

a. The new Bolshevik government was called the _____.

b. A _____ is a Bolshevik or Communist party official who leads a _____ unit, teaches party _____, or preserves party _____.

c. Lenin became the _____ of the new government.

d. Lenin immediately issued decrees to withdraw Russia from _____ and abolish all private _____.

e. On November 9, Lenin shut down anti-Bolshevik _____.

f. _____ returned to Petrograd with an army to _____ the Bolshevik revolution.

g. On November 12, the Bolshevik Red Guards defeated _____'s army at Pulkovo Hills.

h. On November 19, Lenin proclaimed the triumph of the "_____ and _____ revolution."

i. On November 25, the planned _____ for the constituent assembly were held.

j. The Bolsheviks won only _____ percent of the delegates in the assembly.

29. What did Lenin do to make sure the Bolsheviks controlled the government? Why does this show that the new government was not really the "people's" government nor democratic? *(pg. 506)*

_____

_____

_____

_____

_____

30. *True or false? (pgs. 507 – 508)*

a. _____ President Wilson thought Benedict XV's peace plan was impractical.

b. _____ Wilson's "Fourteen Points" for peace were very different from Benedict XV's Seven Points for peace.

c. _____ Wilson called for an increase in armaments to protect world peace.

d. _____ Wilson agreed with Benedict that there should be an international institution to settle disputes between nations.

e. _____ Wilson and Benedict both called for new states based on national identity.

f. _____ Wilson wanted the breakup the Austro-Hungarian Empire into independent states, based on nationality.

g. _____ Wilson did not think a multinational empire could be democratic.

h. _____ Emperor Karl of Austria refused to consider Wilson's peace plan.

i. _____ Germany did not accept all of Wilson's proposals.

j. _____ Allied peace plans were based on the belief that the Central Powers were losing the war.

31. *Answer the following. (pg. 509)*

a. When did the war on the Eastern Front end? _____

b. What was the name of the treaty that ended fighting between Russia and Germany? _____

c. What areas did Russia agree to give Germany by the treaty? _____

d. What countries did Russia agree to evacuate? _____

e. How did the Bolsheviks benefit from the treaty? _____

_____

f. Give two great benefits the treaty brought to the Central Powers:

    • _____

    • _____

g. What did Germany think was its chief danger in 1918? _____

_____

_____

32. Complete these words of General Haig to his British troops as they fought Germany in its last great offensive on the Western Front: *(pg. 509)*

"There must be no _____. With our backs

to the _____... each one of us must

_____."

33. *Answer the following. (pgs. 510 – 511)*

a. Why was the Austrian army at a disadvantage as it faced the Italian army in June 1918?

_____

_____

_____

b. Who won the Battle of the Piave River? _____

c. How did the Battle of the Piave River change the war for the Austrians? _____

_____

d. Was Ludendorff's *Friedensturm* on the Western Front a success or failure? _____

e. What battle turned the tide of the war? _____

f. Finish this quote from Germany's Chancellor:

"On the eighteenth, even the most optimistic among

us knew that _____.

The history of the world was _____

_____."

34. *Answer the following. (pgs. 511 – 516)*

a. Give two reasons why the German war effort began collapsing in the second half of 1918:

- _____

- _____

b. Describe the situation in Germany:

_____

_____

c. What was the result of the massive Allied attack against the Germans at Amiens?

_____

_____

_____

d. What did President Wilson demand of Germany as conditions to ending the war?

_____

_____

_____

e. What reform did Emperor Karl propose in the "People's Manifesto"?

_____

_____

_____

f. What was President Wilson's response to the People's Manifesto?

_____

_____

_____

g. Why did Emperor Karl refuse to abdicate?

_____

_____

h. What did Emperor Karl do instead of abdicating? What was his reason?

_____

_____

i. What did Emperor Karl approve on November 11, 1918?

_____

j. What did Karl ask the people of German-Austria to do? _____

_____

k. Complete this quote from Emperor Karl:

> "The _____ of my people has, from the beginning, been the object of my most ardent wishes. Only an inner _____ can heal the _____ of this war.

l. Explain how the reign of Kaiser Wilhelm came to an end: _____

_____

_____

_____

_____

m. Why didn't the Allies last great offensive planned for November 14 ever happen?

_____

_____

> **The guns fell silent all along the Western Front at _____ on _____**
>
> **"the _____ hour of the _____ day of the _____ month"**

Chapter 18: The Rise of Totalitarian Regimes

1. *Complete the following. (pgs. 521 – 522)*

a. What tragic event occurred in Siberia about midnight on July 16-17, 1918?

_____

_____

_____

_____

_____

b. Finish this quote from Trotsky about the event:

"The severity of this summary justice showed the world that we would _____

_____ "

c. List five groups that were enemies of Lenin and his Bolsheviks: _____

_____

d. What were the anti-Bolshevik counterrevolutionaries called? _____

e. What foreign powers aided the counterrevolutionaries? _____

f. What was the Bolshevik army formed to fight the counterrevolutionaries called? _____

g. Give **four** reasons so many Russians who were not Bolsheviks fought against the counterrevolutionaries:

- _____

- _____

- _____

- _____

h. By 1920, which side was victorious in the civil war in Russia? _____

i. What two events in August 1918 caused the Bolsheviks to initiate the "Red Terror"? *(pgs. 522 – 523)*

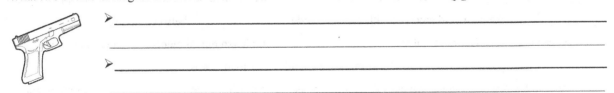

➢ _____

_____

➢ _____

_____

j. Finish this quote: *(pg. 523)*

"For every drop of _____ blood there will be shed a _____ of the blood of those who oppose the _____ and the proletariat leaders."

2. *In each statement below* <u>cross out</u> *the ending phrase that would make the statement* <u>*false*</u>*. (pgs. 523 – 524)*

a. The Bolsheviks used the Red Terror to …

> … safeguard the revolution and terrorize anyone who opposed it.
> … destroy the foes of the proletariat.
> … protect the bourgeoisie.
> … hold on to their power in government.

b. During the Red Terror…

> … supporters of the old tsarist government were executed.
> … the proletariat class was exterminated.
> … striking workers were killed in mass executions.
> … at least 140,000 Russians were killed.

c. The Cheka was …

> … the chief instrument used to carry out the Red Terror.
> … the Extraordinary Commission for the Battle against Counter-Revolutionary Sabotage and Speculation.
> … a police force created by Robespierre.
> … given absolute power to arrest, judge, condemn, and execute counterrevolutionary suspects.

d. The Bolshevik government claimed …

> … it received its authority from God.
> … it had the right to do whatever was necessary to save the revolution.
> … it had the absolute right to abolish any and all rights and freedoms.
> … it had absolute power and authority over the total life of society and individuals.

e. The Bolshevik government could be described as…

> … democratic.   … totalitarian.   … oppressive.   … authoritarian.   …. brutal.

3. *Fill in the blanks. (pgs. 524 – 526)*

a. The Great War officially ended with the signing of the Treaty of

_____ on June _____, _____.

b. The peace treaty was drawn up by the "Big _____" which included

President _____ of the United States, Prime

Minster David Lloyd George of _____, Premier

Georges Clemenceau of _____, and Prime Minister Vittorio Orlando of _____.

c. _____ convinced the Allies to include in the treaty an approval for the formation of a League of

_____, which would have the authority to decide _____ between nations.

d. Clemenceau and Lloyd George wanted _____ and harsh punishments against Germany, but

_____ kept it from being even harsher than it was.

e. Even though the treaty was not as harsh as it could have been it was still a great _____ to Germany and

made it no longer a great _____.

f. According to the terms of the treaty:

   ➢ Germany had to admit that the _____ were entirely responsible for the war.

   ➢ Germany had to accept responsibility for the _____ and _____ to the Allies.

   ➢ Germany had to pay the Allies _____ billion by May 1921.

   ➢ The Allied armies would _____ the lands between Germany's western border and the _____ River to make sure that Germany fulfilled her obligations.

   ➢ Germany could not have an army of over _____ men.

   ➢ Germany could not keep _____ or maintain _____ anywhere within a strip running _____ miles east of the Rhine.

   ➢ Germany lost most of West _____, which was given to _____.

   ➢ Germany had to give _____ 15-year economic control of the Saar Basin, a region with much industry and _____.

   ➢ Germany was forced to abandon all her overseas _____ and was deprived of much of her wealth in _____, _____, and other _____ used in industry.

   ➢ Germany lost _____ square miles of territory and 6 _____ of its population.

g. After the war, the former Habsburg Empire was restructured by the Allies:

   • It was divided into three _____ states: Austria, _____ and _____.

   • Austria had to give Trentino and her territory on the Adriatic to _____.

   • Austria had to give _____ and Herzegovina to the kingdom of _____ (Serbia).

   • Bohemia and Slovakia were joined to the independent republic of _____.

   • Hungary had to give Croatia and Slavonia to _____.

   • Romania received _____ and other lands that were formerly part of Hungary.

h. Since most Austrians spoke _____, Austrians hoped they could be united to _____.

i. Wilson and the Allies did not want the countries to be united since Austria's population was _____ and they feared the united countries would be under the control of the _____.

4. Describe what happened to Emperor Karl. *(pg. 527)*

   _____

   _____

   _____

   _____

   _____

   _____

   _____

   _____

5. *Number the events in Hungary in the order they happened. (pgs. 526 – 528)*

a. _____ To crush opposition, Kun initiated his own Red Terror similar to Russia's.

b. _____ In Budapest, Kun published a Bolshevik newspaper in which he criticized the Liberal government.

c. _____ In June 1920, Hungary signed a peace treaty with the Allies.

d. _____ When the Romanians withdrew from Budapest, Horthy entered and restored the kingdom of Hungary.

e. __1__ Near the end of World War I, the government of Hungary fell into anarchy.

f. _____ In December 1918, Lenin sent Bela Kun – a Hungarian Jew and Bolshevik – to Budapest with a large amount of money to organize a revolution.

g. _____ On March 1, 1920, Horthy was elected regent and claimed to rule in the name of Emperor Karl.

h. _____ Kun was imprisoned but continued to spread Bolshevik propaganda and organize a Communist Party.

i. _____ Admiral Miklos Horthy led the Hungarian counterrevolutionaries in a brutal "White Terror."

j. _____ When Kun was released from prison, he organized a coalition government with the socialists.

k. _____ The Romanians marched on Budapest and Kun fled to Vienna on August 1.

l. _____ On March 1919, Kun proclaimed the Hungarian Soviet Republic.

m. _____ All moderate socialists were removed from the government and Kun became dictator of Hungary.

n. _____ In 1921, Emperor Karl tried to reestablish his rule in Hungary, but failed.

6. *Answer the following. (pgs. 528 – 530)*

a. On what idea did the Allied powers base their redrawing of boundaries is Central and Eastern Europe?

_____

_____

b. What mistaken assumption did the Allies have about Central and Eastern Europe?

_____

_____

c. Give **three** reasons why the Allied plan to form new nation-states proved difficult:

- _____
- _____
- _____

d. What made the newly formed countries of Central Europe weak and unstable?

_____

_____

e. What **five** new independent states were formed in northeastern Europe after the Great War?

_____

f. Circle the countries above in "e" that successfully established democratic governments.

g. Underline the countries above in "e" that were small and weak.

7. *Complete the following. (pgs. 530 – 532)*

a. What were the causes of Russia's famine and poverty after its civil war? *Check the correct statements.*

____ Lenin seized the produce of peasant farms to feed workers in the cities.

____ Peasants decided not to grow anything the government would not pay them for, so less food was grown.

____ Russia shipped large amounts of produce to Central Europe as part of war reparations.

____ The counterrevolutionaries had destroyed many factories in the major cities.

____ Since the government did not train workers to manage factories, industrial production declined dramatically.

____ Russia lost a great deal of productive land as part of the Treaty of Versailles.

____ Russian peasants were not ready for the radical policies of the Bolshevik government.

b. What were some points of Lenin's New Economic Policy (NEP)? *Check the correct statements.*

____ The Red Army would retake Poland, Lithuania, Estonia, Latvia, and Finland.

____ Instead of giving all surplus produce to the government, peasants would pay a tax.

____ Small factories would be privately owned.

____ The government would control large and middle-sized factories.

____ Lenin would renegotiate the Treaty of Versailles.

____ More workers in the cities would be relocated to the country to become farmers.

c. By 1922, which territories were under Russian rule? *Circle the correct names.*

Armenia   Azerbaijan   Estonia   Finland   Georgia   Lithuania   Poland   Siberia   Ukraine

d. Fill in the blanks to show the federal union the Russian congress formed in the new constitution of 1922:

_____ of Soviet Socialist Republics

(or _____)

_____ Soviet Federative Socialist Republic

_____ Soviet Federative Socialist Republic

_____ Soviet Socialist Republic

_____ Soviet Socialist Republic

e. What were the characteristics of Russia's new government? *Check the correct statements.*

____ The constitution accurately described how the government worked in reality.

____ It was democratic because it gave the suffrage to all working men and women, ages 18 and older.

____ Each republic had its own independent government.

____ Each republic sent representatives to the union's central government in Moscow.

____ Landowners, employers, and clergy were forbidden to vote.

____ All government officials were directly elected by the people.

____ Voters could not be intimidated to vote for the "right" candidate.

____ The central government held almost all political power.

____ The Communist Party was the only legal party in Russia.

____ It was under the complete control of the Communist Party and its chairman.

____ The chairman of the Communist Party was elected by the Russian people.

Did you know? The joined hammer and sickle is the symbol of the Communist Party. The sickle is a sharp tool that was used to cut and harvest grain by peasants. The hammer was a tool used in industry by city workers. The union of the two items is meant to represent the proletariat or working class.

8. *Answer the following. (pgs. 532 – 533)*

a. What did Lenin demand of members of the Communist Party? _____

_____

_____

b. Describe the "Communist paradise" where all workers were to be led: _____

_____

_____

c. Write **two** ways the Communist Party used to disseminate its ideas and to crush opposition:

- _____

- _____

d. Explain why Communists called religion the "opiate of the people." _____

_____

_____

e. Write **six** ways the Communists persecuted the Russian Orthodox and Catholic Churches:

- _____

- _____

- _____

- _____

- _____

- _____

f. What was Lenin's dream? _____

_____

g. Why are Communists called universalists? _____

_____

_____

h. Write two differences between the Trotsky faction and the Stalin faction in the Communist Party:

- _____

_____

- _____

_____

Did you know? After Lenin died, his body was embalmed to preserve it for public display. His body rests in a glass sarcophagus in a mausoleum in Moscow. A team of scientists monitor the condition of Lenin's corpse and every 18 months it is taken to a lab for re-embalming. "Lenin's Mausoleum" in Red Square is a red and black monument made of marble and concrete and shaped like an ancient step pyramid.

9. In each box write an important fact about Stalin or a word or phrase to describe him. *(pgs. 533 – 534)*

10. *Number the events in Stalin's rise to power in the order they happened. (pgs. 533 – 534)*

a. ____ In Petrograd, Stalin organized soviets and helped rebuild the Bolshevik party.

b. ____ On January 21, 1924, Lenin died.

c. _1_ Stalin became an active socialist and was arrested by the tsarist government and exiled to Siberia.

d. ____ Trotsky and other powerful Communists tried to oust Stalin from the party's leadership.

e. ____ Stalin joined the Bolshevik party and escaped from Siberia in 1904.

f. ____ In April 1929, the Communist Party confirmed Stalin as the dictator of the USSR.

g. ____ In May 1922, Lenin suffered his first stroke and became less active in the government.

h. ____ Stalin was freed from exile in 1917 and returned to Petrograd.

i. ____ In 1928, Stalin expelled Trotsky and about 80 other Communists from Russia.

j. ____ After escaping from arrest five times, Stalin was sent to Siberia in 1913.

k. ____ In early 1922, Stalin was elected the general secretary of the party and became very powerful.

l. ____ After Lenin's death, the party split into two factions – one led by Trotsky; the other, by Stalin.

m. ____ In 1925, the party forced Trotsky to resign as commissar for war and removed Trotsky's followers from the army and navy.

11. *Complete the following. (pg. 534)*

a. What does "collectivize" mean? _____

_____

b. What did Stalin do when the wealthy peasants (*kulaks*) resisted his order to collectivize?

_____

_____

_____

c. Write four ways Stalin intensified the persecution of the Orthodox Church:

- _____

- _____

- _____

- _____

12. In each box write an important fact about Mussolini or a word or phrase to describe him. *(pg. 535)*

13. *In each statement below* <u>cross out</u> *the ending phrase that would make the statement* <u>*false*</u>. *(pgs. 535 – 536)*

a. After the Great War, Italians were dissatisfied because…

> … the cost of living had greatly increased.
> … returning soldiers could not find jobs.
> … the war had not made Italy a great power in the eastern Mediterranean.
> … Italy had lost much land in the Treaty of London.

b. Italy's hardships caused the people to…

> … lose trust in the king and the Liberal government.
> … elect socialists to seats in government.
> … murder Bolshevik party members.
> … support proletariat revolution and worker strikes.

c. The Fascist Party formed by Benito Mussolini was…

> … named after the ancient Roman *fasces*.
> … backed by rich businessmen and local landowners.
> … extremely nationalistic and anti-socialist.
> … committed to nonviolence to achieve its goals.

d. Mussolini gained control of the government and became prime minister…

> … through the help of the "Blackshirts."
> … through a clever election campaign.
> … because the king and his government did nothing to stop him.
> … after the Fascists used violence to overcome opposition.

e. Many Italians supported Mussolini because…

> … they were tired of the strikes and unrest in Italy.
> … they thought he could bring peace, prosperity, and glory to Italy.
> … he promised to fight for workers' rights.
> … the Fascists intimidated voters.

14. What is the item pictured on this page called? Why did you think the Fascists adopted it as their party symbol?

_____

_____

_____

_____

15. There are similarities and differences between Mussolini's Fascism in Italy and Bolshevik Communism in Russia. *Read each statement below, then decided what regime it describes. If it describes Fascist Italy, write "FI" on the line. If it describes Bolshevik Russia, write "BR" on the line. If it describes both regimes, leave the line blank. (pgs. 537 – 538)*

a. _____ Every person and institution is the servant of the state.

b. _____ Private property was abolished.

c. _____ The government used skillful propaganda to win support for its policies.

d. _____ It was a totalitarian state.

e. _____ It was nationalist, wanting to be the greatest in the world.

f. _____ A group of secret police kept the public under close supervision.

g. _____ It was anti-Liberal, but not anti-socialist.

h. _____ It tried to destroy religion and the Church.

i. _____ It worked to spread world-wide revolution.

j. _____ It was imperialistic.

k. _____ All opposition parties were outlawed.

l. _____ Businesses were not owned by the government, but they were not independent from the government either.

m. _____ The party formed organizations for youth to indoctrinate them in party principles.

n. _____ Only people who swore to uphold the government could teach in schools and universities.

o. _____ It wanted to be the greatest nation in the world.

p. _____ Freedom of speech was abolished.

q. _____ There should be a one-class proletariat society.

r. _____ It was anti-Catholic but tried to make peace with the Church.

s. _____ The head of the party controlled the government.

t. _____ Government is not founded to protect human liberty.

u. _____ It was anti-Liberal and anti-socialist.

v. _____ The economy was not based on *laissez-faire* capitalism.

w. _____ Factories and businesses were confiscated and run by the government.

x. _____ It was internationalist, rejecting the domination of one nation by another.

y. _____ Different classes are a natural part of human society.

z. _____ Different industries were organized into corporations made up of both employers and employees.

Study Skills: *Organizing information in different ways can help you understand things better. Another way to do the above exercise is with a Venn diagram. On a separate sheet of paper, draw two large overlapping circles like the ones illustrated below. In the shared area between the two circles, write the similarities between Fascism and Communism. In the separate areas, write the differences. Write only a few words or phrases from the sentences above in the circles.*

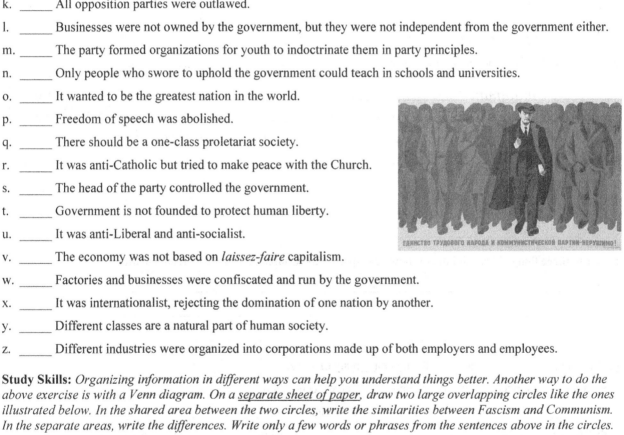

16. *Complete the following. (pgs. 538 – 541)*

a. Write the motto of Pope Pius XI:

> [blank box]

b. Complete this quote from Pius XI's encyclical *Ubi Arcano Dei Consilio*:

> "In the face of our much praised _____, we behold
> with sorrow society _____ back slowly but surely
> into a state of _____."

c. Write **four** reasons Pius XI gave to explain why there was still not true peace in the world:

- _____
- _____
- _____
- _____

d. Complete Pius XI's thoughts about peace:

> Because of human _____, no human _____ by itself can bring
> peace. True peace can only come through _____ and _____, which are
> the fruits of the _____, communicated through his _____.

e. What was the "Roman Question"? _____
_____
_____

f. Write **three** things Mussolini did to show he respected the Church and wanted a reconciliation:

- _____
- _____
- _____

g. Complete the important points of the <u>Lateran Treaty</u> of 1929:

- ❖ It created an independent state of about _____ acres, centered on _____
- ❖ The _____ would be the independent sovereign of this "_____" state.
- ❖ This city would have its own _____, _____ system, _____ transmission, and _____
- ❖ The pope could make _____ with other nations, even if Italy were at _____ with them.
- ❖ The Italian _____ paid an _____ to the pope for the seizure of the Papal States in 1870.
- ❖ The pope recognized the Italian kingdom as a _____

h. Complete the important points of the concordat between the Holy See and the Italian state:

❖ Italy declared the "Holy, Catholic, Apostolic, and Roman Religion" to be the only _____ religion.

❖ Italy pledged that all future _____ would be guided by Catholic _____ teaching.

❖ Italy recognized _____ as a sacrament.

❖ Italy agreed to make religious instruction _____ in elementary and secondary schools.

❖ Religion teachers were to be chosen by the _____ and supported by the _____.

❖ Catholic _____, such as Catholic Action, could act without any _____ from the state.

i. Write **four** ways Mussolini violated the concordat:

● _____

● _____

● _____

● _____

j. What did Pius XI do in response to the Fascist persecution of the Church? _____

_____

_____

k. Why did Mussolini pull back on his attacks against the Church? _____

_____

_____

17. *Match the columns. You may need a dictionary.*

A. Blackshirts

B. *Il Duce*

C. Politburo

D. Man of Steel

E. indoctrinate

F. propaganda

G. internationalism

H. imperialistic

I. Benedict XV

J. Pius XI

K. Vittorio Emanuele III

L. *Ubi Arcano Dei Consilio*

M. *Non Abbiamo Bisogno*

N. Catholic Action

O. Lateran Treaty

[ ] powerless king of Italy during the Fascist take-over of the Italian government

[ ] pope who reigned during World War I

[ ] organization of laymen who tried to influence society with Catholic ideals

[ ] 1929 agreement between the Holy See and the Italian government

[ ] information spread deliberately to further a cause or to damage an opposing cause

[ ] Pius XI's first encyclical, in which he explained the goals of his papacy

[ ] Stalin's pseudonym

[ ] central committee of the Russian Communist Party

[ ] armed squads of Italian Fascists, loyal to Mussolini

[ ] title given to Mussolini; Italian for "the leader"

[ ] to instruct in fundamental ideas (it has a negative meaning of one-sided instruction)

[ ] cooperation among nations to achieve a common good

[ ] first ruler of the Vatican City

[ ] desire to conquer other nations in order to form a great empire

[ ] papal encyclical which criticized the principles of fascism and Mussolini's anti-Catholic actions

18. Write **three** challenges that faced the Weimar Republic after the war: *(pg. 542)*

- _____
  _____
- _____
  _____
- _____
  _____

19. *Circle the word or phrase in bold that correctly completes each statement. (pg. 542)*

a. Germany's new constitution was signed at **[Berlin/Weimar]** and created a **[democratic/authoritarian]** republic.

b. **[Male/All]** adult citizens could vote in Germany's new government.

c. The **[Social Democrats/Communists]** held the most seats in the elected assembly.

d. Members of the Catholic Center Party and the **[Democrats/Republicans]** also won seats in the assembly.

e. **[Executive/Legislative]** power was shared by a president and a chancellor.

f. The president was elected every **[four/seven]** years and the chancellor was appointed by the **[Reichsrat/president]**.

g. The central government had a two-house National Assembly, which **(made laws/enforced laws)** for the country.

h. Members of the National Assembly's *Reichstag* were **[elected by the citizens/appointed by the chancellor]**.

i. Members of the National Assembly's *Reichsrat* were **[elected by the citizens/appointed by the states]**.

j. Germany's new government was one of the **[least/most]** democratic governments in Europe, but it was very **[weak/strong]**.

20. *Number the events in the order they happened. (pgs. 543 – 544)*

a. _____ In December 1922, the Allies declared Germany in default.

b. _____ Resisting Germans were fined and imprisoned and lost their jobs and property.

c. _____ Germany announced that it could not make its yearly reparation payment of $500 million.

d. _____ In August 1924, the Dawes Committee came up with a new payment plan for Germany that included a loan and a significant reduction in reparation payments.

e. _15_ Germany's economy began to recover.

f. _1_ After World War I, the German mark experienced inflation and the Germany economy collapsed.

g. _____ The German government could not get any loans from foreign countries.

h. _____ The German chancellor called for peaceful resistance to the French and Belgian occupation.

i. _____ In July 1922, Germany asked for another moratorium, but the Allies did not grant one.

j. _____ In late 1924, Germany began making reparation payments and the occupying troops withdrew from the Ruhr.

k. _____ Germany again said it could not make the payments.

l. _____ French and Belgian troops occupied the highly industrialized Ruhr district in northwest Germany.

m. _____ In October 1923, the new German chancellor ordered an end to the resistance in the Ruhr district and asked the Allies to come up with a plan that would help Germany make its reparation payments.

n. _____ Seeing that the resistance had no effect, Germans began to turn against the Weimar Republic.

o. _____ The Allies granted Germany a temporary moratorium on payments.

21. Give **three** reasons why Germany's economic recovery was not as strong as it seemed in 1929: *(pg. 544)*

- _____

- _____

- _____

22. *In each box, write an important fact about Adolf Hitler. (pg. 545)*

23. *Match the columns. (pgs. 543 – 546)*

A. inflation   [   ] failure to fulfill an obligation

B. moratorium   [   ] the Holy Roman Empire

C. default   [   ] white, European race

D. Nazis   [   ] Nazis private army; "storm troopers"

E. *Führer*   [   ] book Hitler wrote in prison which explains his political ideas

F. Adolf Hitler   [   ] the empire of Bismarck's Germany

G. *Schutzstaffeln (SS)*   [   ] people of an ethnic group

H. *Sturmarbeilung*   [   ] decrease in the value of money, which leads to a rise in prices for goods

I. *Mein Kampf*   [   ] "leader"

J. volk   [   ] German empire formed by Hitler

K. Aryan   [   ] delay

L. First Reich   [   ] National Socialists German Workers' Party

M. Second Reich   [   ] Nazis "protection squadron"

N. Third Reich   [   ] leader of the National Socialists German Workers' Party

Did you know? The Nazis adopted as their symbol a black swastika in a white circle against a red background. The word *swastika* is not German, but Sanskrit. It is an ancient symbol, often religious, seen throughout the world. The different cultures that used the symbol had different explanations for the crossed "arms." For instance, Buddhists said they represented the footprints of Buddha. The ancient Greeks, Romans, and Germanic tribes described them as the lightning bolts of Zeus or Jupiter or Thor. Some cultures used the symbol to represent the sun or eternal movement or eternal life. The swastika has even been found in the Americas among the Aztecs and Navajo (who called it "whirling logs") and other Native American tribes. Because of the Nazis, the swastika is now seen as a negative image.

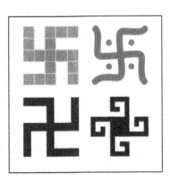

24. *Answer the following. (pgs. 545 – 546)*

a. Why did Hitler despise socialism? _____

_____

b. Why did Hitler hate Jews? _____

_____

c. Why did Hitler reject Christianity? _____

_____

d. Explain Hitler's ideas about race: _____

_____

_____

_____

e. Give **three** promises that Hitler made about the Third Reich:

- _____

- _____

- _____

25. *Number the events of Hitler's rise to power in the order they happened. (pgs. 546 – 548)*

a. ____ In 1932, Hitler ran for president against General Paul von Hindenburg.

b. ____ In the new elections, the Nazis won a larger number of seats in the *Reichstag*.

c. _1_ Through his skills as a speaker and fund-raiser, Hitler became the leader of the Nazi party.

d. ____ Hindenburg refused and dissolved the *Reichstag*.

e. ____ Through propaganda and violence, the Nazis slowly spread Hitler's ideas.

f. ____ Fearing the Communists would take control of the government, Hindenburg's allies began supporting Hitler.

g. ____ In the election of March 1933, the Nazi party gained control of the *Reichstag*.

h. ____ In August 1934, President Hindenburg died and Hitler became president as well as chancellor.

i. ____ Germans turned toward extremist parties on the right and on the left.

j. ____ On April 1, 1933, Hitler demanded he be given the powers of a dictator for four years.

k. ____ In the election of 1930, the Nazi party won 18 percent of the vote.

l. ____ Hindenburg was persuaded that Hitler was harmless and on January 30, 1933, he appointed Hitler chancellor.

m. _7_ Hitler lost the election, but the Nazi party won more seats in the *Reichstag*.

n. _18_ The *Reichstag* agreed to give Hitler absolute power in Germany.

o. ____ Hitler demanded that Hindenburg make him chancellor.

p. ____ Nazi propaganda caused the public to fear a Bolshevik revolution and to support the Nazi party.

q. ____ Hitler and his storm troopers purged the government of opponents and spread the Nazi message.

r. ____ In the next election, the Nazis lost 5 percent of the vote, while the Communists gained more seats.

s. ____ In 1934, the Reichstag transferred the powers of the German states to the central government.

t. ____ In 1929, a great financial crash hit the world and Germany's economy collapsed.

26. Answer the following. *(pgs. 548 - 550)*

a. Write **five** ways Hitler's regime was similar to Mussolini's:

- _____
- _____
- _____
- _____
- _____

b. Write **five** laws Hitler's government enacted against the Jews:

- _____
- _____
- _____
- _____
- _____

c. Write **five** reasons the Catholic Church was a powerful force in postwar Germany:

- _____
- _____
- _____
- _____
- _____

d. What was Hitler's goal regarding the Catholic Church? _____
_____

e. Why did Hitler think this would be a difficult goal to achieve? _____
_____
_____

f. What did some Catholic bishops think was the best way to deal with the Nazi government?
_____
_____

g. Why did a few theologians encourage Catholics to get involved with the Nazi government?
_____
_____

h. What was Hitler's attitude about religion? _____
_____
_____

i. Why did Pope Pius XI sign a concordat with Germany in 1933? _____

_____

j. Write **four** terms of the concordat between the Holy See and Germany:

- _____

- _____

- _____

- _____

k. Why did some people criticize the concordat? _____

_____

l. What was the Church's response to this criticism? _____

_____

_____

_____

_____

m. Write **four** ways Hitler violated the concordat:

- _____

- _____

- _____

- _____

n. Write **four** ways the Nazi government tried to draw Catholics away from the Church:

- _____

- _____

- _____

- _____

o. How did the Nazis take over all education in Germany? _____

_____

_____

_____

p. What did Nazis encourage schoolchildren to do? _____

_____

q. What happened to priests and other Christian ministers who spoke out against Nazi paganism?

_____

_____

Name _____ Date _____

27. *Complete these sentences. (pgs. 551 – 552)*

a. Hitler thought the greatest obstacle to the triumph of National Socialism in Germany was _____.

b. From 1933 to 1937, Hitler faced steady opposition from _____, _____, and _____ , both inside and outside of Germany.

c. _____ and Catholics joined together to oppose Hitler.

d. In 1933, the _____ bishops issued a pastoral letter condemning extreme _____ and anti-_____.

e. In his Christmas message of 1930, Pope Pius XI condemned _____, saying no _____ is superior to another.

f. The Vatican _____, *L'Osservatore Romano*, published criticisms of the Nazi theory of _____, _____, and _____.

g. In 1936, Vatican Radio began exhorting Catholics worldwide to _____.

h. In 1937, Pope Pius XI issued his great _____ of National Socialism in the encyclical,

_____.

i. Besides condemning Nazi ideas, the encyclical called on the German bishops to _____ and encouraged German Catholics to _____.

j. The encyclical was written in _____ and _____ into Germany, where it was secretly _____.

k. The encyclical was delivered by hand to _____, who read it aloud during _____ on Passion Sunday, March 14, 1937.

l. By evening of the same day, police had _____ every copy of the encyclical in Germany.

m. The encyclical did not mention _____ or the _____ by name, but everyone knew who the pope was referring to.

n. Hitler was _____ when he learned of the encyclical and he swore _____ on Pius and the Catholic Church.

Chapter 19: An Even Greater War

1. *Complete the following. (pgs. 557 – 558)*

a. Write the names of **three** political parties vying for power in Austria:

_____   _____   _____

b. Using the names you wrote above, write which political party held each of the following ideas (use acronyms):

_____ Preserve the traditions of Catholic Austria.

_____ Overturn the capitalist system to bring about justice for the working class.

_____ Remove all religious influence from society.

_____ Bring an end to Austrian independence and become part of Germany.

_____ Fight against the injustices of the rich against the lower classes.

_____ Abolish private property.

c. Write the names of the two papal encyclicals that condemned *laissez-faire* capitalism and socialism:

_____   _____

d. What was Chancellor Engelbert Dollfuss's vision for Austria, based on these encyclicals? *Fill in the blanks.*

Dollfuss favored a society made up of mostly small _____, _____, _____,

and _____, not _____ businesses. Each group would be organized into a _____

or _____ that looked out for members and their _____, made sure they

received a _____ or charged a _____for their goods, and protected their

_____. The _____ role would be to make sure that all the various groups worked in

_____ with one another and that the strong _____

e. Explain why Dollfuss thought preserving Austria's peasantry was so important?

_____

_____

_____

f. What was the new threat that faced Dollfuss in 1933? _____

_____

Did you know? Probably the most well-known Austrians of the 20th century were the members of the Trapp family. The Trapps were a large Catholic family from Salzburg who became famous for the beautiful music they sang together. Maria von Trapp, wrote the story of their adventures in *The Story of the Trapp Family Singers* (the basis for the movie *The Sound of Music*). In Maria's book there are descriptions of life in Austria as well its peasant and Catholic customs. Maria and her family lived in Austria while Dollfuss was chancellor, and in her book she describes the political upheaval in her beloved country during that time, as well as her own family's dealings with the Nazis.

2. *In each statement below <u>cross out</u> the ending phrase that would make the statement false. (pgs. 558 – 560)*

a. Dollfuss became dictator of Austria because…

> … he wanted to protect the independence of his country.
> … he was opposed to democracy and parliamentary government.
> … he believed the *Nationalrat* was too weak to deal with Germany.
> … he wanted to keep Austria from becoming socialist.

b. To save Austria from being taken over by Hitler, Dollfuss…

> … sought and received aid from Great Britain and France.
> … abolished Austria's republican government and established an authoritarian government.
> … formed an alliance with Fascist Italy.
> … outlawed the Nazi party in Austria.

c. Dollfuss tried to break the power of the Social Democrats because…

> … its members were armed and ready for revolution.
> … they were not a reliable ally against Nazism.
> … they threatened Austria's independence and its Catholic culture.
> … they had allied themselves with Mussolini.

d. The civil war between the Austrian government and the Social Democrats…

> … started with the assassination of Dollfuss.
> … was a bloody victory for the government.
> … caused the socialists to go underground.
> … caused an increase in Nazi terror attacks throughout Austria.

3. *Complete the following. (pgs. 560 – 562)*

a. Finish each sentence to show how Hitler violated the Treaty of Versailles.

On March 16, 1935, Hitler announced that _____

_____

In March 1936, Hitler moved troops _____

In October 1936, Hitler issued a public repudiation of _____

_____

b. What did the Allies do after Hitler broke each provision of the treaty? _____

_____

c. Explain how Hitler and Mussolini become allies: _____

_____

_____

_____

_____

d. How did this alliance affect Austria? _____

_____

e. What other country entered into a pact with Germany in 1936? _____

Name _____ Date _____

4. *Number the events in the order they happened to show how Austria became Hitler's first conquest.* *(pgs. 562 – 563)*

a. _____ The next day, Hitler proclaimed that Austria was now part of Germany.

b. _____ On March 12, 1938, Hitler led German troops into Austria.

c. _1_ Austria realized it would get no help from France or Great Britain to protect its independence.

d. _____ Schuschnigg did both.

e. _____ Despite the agreement, Austrian Nazis continued to cause unrest in Austria.

f. _____ In a plebiscite on April 10, 99 percent of the Austrians voted in favor of *Anschluss* with Germany, confirming Hitler's claim that he was the "liberator" of Austria.

g. _____ On March 11, 1938, Hitler told Schuschnigg to postpone the plebiscite and resign from office.

h. _____ Chancellor Kurt von Schuschnigg decided he had no choice but to enter into an agreement with Germany.

i. _____ Schuschnigg scheduled a plebiscite for the Austrians to vote on whether they favored *Anschluss* with Germany.

j. _____ In January 1938, Schuschnigg learned that Austrian Nazis were planning to overthrow his government.

k. _____ In July 1936, Schuschnigg agreed to call Austria a "German state" and to legalize the Nazi party if Hitler would respect Austria's independence.

l. _____ Schuschnigg confronted Hitler with the evidence, but Hitler made it clear he supported the insurgents.

m. _____ After the *Anschluss*, SS soldiers arrested and imprisoned tens of thousands of Hitler's political opponents as well as Jews.

5. Explain how Stalin's "Five-Year Plan" caused the death from starvation of millions of people. *(pgs. 563 – 565)*

6. The *Holodomor* is recognized as a genocide of the Ukrainian people. Look up the definition of "genocide." On a separate sheet of paper describe the *Holodomor* and explain why it called a genocide.

7. *Answer the following. (pgs. 565 – 566)*

a. Was Stalin's first Five-Year Plan to industrialize the Soviet Union quickly successful? _____

b. What were the goals of Stalin's second Five-Year Plan? _____

_____

c. Write **three** benefits of the second Five-Year Plan for the Russian economy:

- _____

- _____

- _____

d. Write **four** improvements to living conditions Stalin's plans brought to the Soviet Union:

- _____

- _____

- _____

- _____

e. Write **three** ways Stalin's government violated its socialist principles to achieve progress:

- _____

- _____

- _____

f. In what ways did Stalin's Russia resemble the capitalist system? _____

_____

_____

8. *Complete the following. (pgs. 567 – 568)*

a. Fill in the blanks to show how Stalin tried to liquidate religion between 1932 and 1937.

The government ordered a round of _____. Some _____ were

destroyed and some _____ were used as granaries or turned into antireligious _____. An atheist

group called the League of the _____ attacked religion in its magazine called "The

_____." The League also mocked religion in traveling _____, _____, and

_____. The government changed _____ so that it went from being

merely _____ to antireligious.

b. What surprised Stalin and the atheists after five years of persecution? _____

_____

_____

_____

> The letters around the Russian Orthodox cross stand for "Jesus Christ conquers."

c. How did Stalin persecute religion after 1937?

_____

_____

_____

_____

d. What three things did Pope Pius XI do in 1930 after condemning the persecution in Russia?

- _____

- _____

- _____

e. What did Pius XI write about Communism in his encyclical *Divini Redemptoris*? (*Fill in the blanks.*)

"The Communism of today strips man of his _____, robs human personality of all its _____, and removes all the _____ that check the eruption of blind _____."

By refusing to life any _____ or _____ character, Communism attacks human _____ and undermines _____ and the _____ and directs everything in society to one purpose - the production of material _____.

"Communism is _____, and no one who would save Christian civilization may _____ with it in any undertaking whatsoever."

f. According to Pius XI, what were three reasons Communism spread so quickly?

- _____

- _____

- _____

g. What do you think Stalin meant when he said contemptuously, "The pope! How many divisions does he have?"

_____

_____

_____

h. What did Stalin begin doing in 1936 to secure his power as leader of the Communist Party?

_____

_____

_____

9. In each box write a sentence to describe Spain at the beginning of the 20th century. *(pg. 569)*

10. *Complete the following. (pgs. 570 – 571)*

a. What kind of government did Spain have at the beginning of the 20th century? *Circle the correct word.*

      absolute monarch   Liberal democracy   constitutional monarchy   democratic republic

b. <u>Underline</u> all the factors that convinced high-ranking military men that Spain needed a military dictatorship:

King Alfonso XIII was cruel and unjust.
Socialists and anarchists were causing unrest.
The Spanish army was defeated by native tribesmen in Morocco.
Workers in industrial centers were striking.
Soldiers coming back from the Great War could not find jobs.
Nationalist groups in the region of Catalonia were demanding to be made an independent state.
The Communist Party had established itself in Spain.

c. Who was chosen as the military dictator of Spain? _____

d. Did King Alfonso remain in power during the military dictatorship? _____

e. Fill in the blanks to show the actions of the military dictator when in power:

He suspended the _____ and dissolved the _____.

He suppressed freedom of _____ and abolished _____.

He brought _____ to Spain in the first five years of his rule and Spain generally prospered.

His government undertook _____ works, such as developing _____ power.

He subdued the rebels in _____.

f. How long did the military dictatorship last and how did it end? _____

_____

_____

g. What did Spaniards demand after the end of the dictatorship? _____

_____

_____

11. *Number the events leading to the Spanish Civil War in the order they happened. (pgs. 571 – 572)*

a. _____ After the election, socialists turned against the government and began to embrace Bolshevik ideas.

b. _____ Zamora was appointed provisional president of a newly established Republic of Spain.

c. _____ Alfonso abdicated and went into exile in France.

d. _____ Fearing that Spain was heading toward Communism, Spanish generals secretly planned a revolt against the government.

e. _____ The new *Cortes* established a secular and anti-church constitution.

f. __1_ On April 12, 1931, republicans won most of the elections to local government offices.

g. _____ In late 1935, Communists and other radical groups formed a coalition called the Popular Front.

h. _____ The murder stirred up fears of a Bolshevik revolution in Spain.

i. _____ In the 1933 elections, the conservatives won the largest number of seats in the *Cortes*.

j. _____ A *junta* of republican leaders declared they would call for a revolution if the King Alfonso did not abdicate.

k. _____ By July 20, 1936, rebel generals and their troops had taken control of Morocco, the Canary Islands, and north-central and northwestern Spain.

l. _____ In the February 1936 elections, the Popular Front won a majority of seats in the *Cortes*.

m. _____ Several generals issued a pronouncement, calling for the overthrow of the government.

n. _____ In the June 1931 elections for the new *Cortes*, the socialists and radical republicans received most of the votes.

o. _____ The traditional and right-wing groups formed a conservative coalition.

p. _17_ The army in Morocco, under the command of General Francisco Franco, rose in revolt.

q. _____ On July 12, 1936, leftist police and Communist militiamen murdered a conservative leader of the *Cortes*.

r. _____ After the election, socialists and anarchists carried out acts of terrorism and street violence in Spanish cities.

12. *Answer the following. (pgs. 571 – 572)*

a. List **five** characteristics of Spain's secular and anti-Church constitution and government:

- _____
- _____
- _____
- _____
- _____

b. Write the name of the right-wing group in CEDA who held the following ideas:

Symbol of CEDA

_____ were nationalistic, favored a highly centralized government, and praised military glory. They thought the Catholic Church was necessary to preserve Spanish culture. They wanted to form Spanish society based on Catholic teachings on social justice and government.

_____ wanted a weaker central government and strong local governments. They opposed the government's anti-Catholic laws and wanted a government based on the social teachings of the Church.

_____ and _____ were chiefly interested in maintaining their power in society. They did not care about workers' rights or improving conditions for poor peasants.

13. *In each statement below <u>cross out</u> the ending phrase that would make the statement false. (pgs. 573 – 575)*

a. During the Spanish Civil War, the Reds…

> … used the military revolt as an opportunity to stage a full-scale socialist revolution.
> … set up their own local governments.
> … were careful not to kill ordinary citizens, but only rebels.
> … killed rebels and their political opponents in cold blood.

b. During the Spanish Civil War, the rebels…

> … shed much blood in the districts they controlled.
> … committed acts of sacrilege and destroyed churches.
> … were better organized and directed by a junta of generals.
> … killed fewer innocent people than the Reds.

c. General Francisco Franco…

> … formed the "International Brigades" to fight the Spanish Communists.
> … was chosen to lead the Nationalist government.
> … organized a military dictatorship that he proclaimed was the rightful government of Spain.
> … united the right-wing groups into a common political party.

d. The Loyalist government in Madrid…

> … became controlled by the Communists.
> … received arms and ammunition from the Soviet Union.
> … was supported by leftist volunteers from other European countries and the U.S.A.
> … established a military dictatorship.

e. The Nationalist government in rebel-controlled Spain …

> … received military aid from Fascist governments.
> … was controlled by the *Falange Española Tradicionalista* political party.
> … received a reputation for bloodthirstiness and cruelty.
> … eventually became controlled by Mussolini and Hitler.

f. The Spanish Civil War…

> … was won by the Nationalists.
> … made Franco dictator of Spain.
> … brought peace and unity to Spain.
> … caused the deaths of hundreds of thousands.

14. Write **two** <u>criticisms</u> and **two** <u>defenses</u> of Franco's authoritarian government: *(pg. 575)*

_____

_____

_____

_____

_____

_____

_____

Name _____ Date _____

15. *Using the map, follow the directions below. (Refer to the maps in Chapter 18 and 19. You may also use an atlas.)*

a. Label these countries: **Austria, Belgium, Czechoslovakia, France, Germany, Great Britain, Hungary, Italy, Lithuania, Netherlands, Poland, Spain, Switzerland, USSR.**

b. <u>Shade in</u> the two countries that Germany added to its *Reich* in 1938 and 1939. *(pgs. 575 – 576)*

c. <u>Draw an **X**</u> on the country that Germany and the USSR divided between themselves in 1939. *(pg. 577)*

d. <u>Draw a line</u> from Italy to the country it invaded and conquered in 1939. *(pg. 576)*

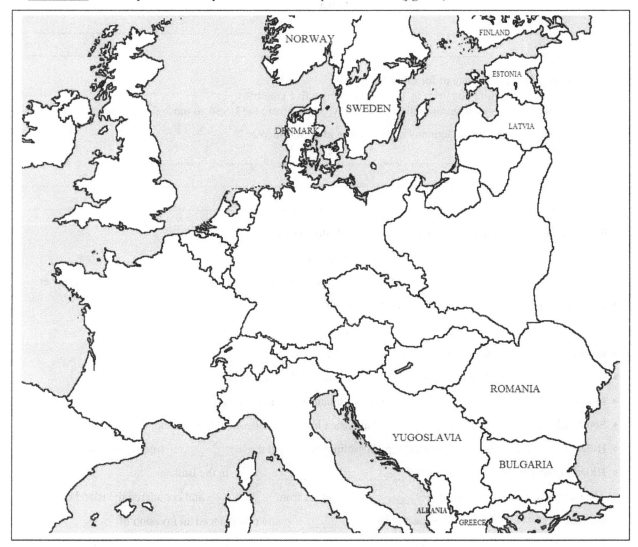

16. *Answer the following. (pgs. 576 – 577)*

a. What was Great Britain's initial strategy to deal with Hitler? _____

_____

b. In the secret agreements between Hitler and Stalin, what did each side get? _____

_____

_____

_____

17. *Complete the following. (pgs. 578 – 580)*

a. What two countries declared war on Germany in 1939? _____

b. What did these countries do to deal with Hitler? _____

_____

c. Explain why the Second World War was truly a world war: _____

_____

_____

d. (Use the map on preceding page of for this exercise.)
    Germany invaded **five** more countries in 1940. Circle those five countries.
    The USSR invaded five countries as well in 1940. Draw arrows from the USSR to those five countries.

e. How did Hitler get revenge for Germany's humiliation after World War I?

_____

_____

_____

f. Fill in the blanks to complete the events of the war in 1940 and 1941:

   • _____ signed an armistice with Germany on June 21, 1940.

   • _____ carried out bombing night raids on German cities throughout the spring and summer.

   • Germany began bombing raids on the coastal towns of _____ in August.

   • Mussolini ordered Italian troops in Libya to invade _____-held _____.

   • Italian troops in Albania invaded _____.

   • In December 1940, British forces in _____ pushed the Italians back into Libya.

   • In January 1941, the _____ drove the Italians back into Albania.

   • South African and other _____ forces in Africa invaded Italian-held Somaliland, Eritrea, and _____.

   • Hitler sent German troops to Africa to help Mussolini and pushed the _____ troops back into _____.

   • Hitler's armies invaded and conquered _____ in the Balkans.

   • The Germans invaded and drove the _____ forces from _____ and conquered the island of _____.

   • On June 22, 1941, Hitler broke his pact with _____ and commenced an invasion of _____.

g. What prevented Hitler from focusing his attention on his war with Great Britain?

_____

_____

h. What are some possible reasons why Hitler turned against Stalin and decided to destroy the Soviets?

_____

_____

_____

_____

18. *Match the columns. (pgs. 575 – 583)*

A. Siegfried Line

B. Maginot Line

C. *Blitzkrieg*

D. Triple Axis

E. Free France

F. RAF

G. Forest of Compiégne

H. Ukraine

I. Pearl Harbor

J. Blue Division

K. Winston Churchill

L. Erwin Rommel

M. Neville Chamberlain

N. Charles De Gaulle

O. Franklin D. Roosevelt

P. Joseph Petain

[   ] Great Britain's prime minister who favored appeasement with Germany

[   ] French general who organized the resistance to the Germans in France

[   ] dictator of southern France after the French surrendered to Germany

[   ] general of the German army

[   ] site of U.S. naval base in Hawaii attacked by Japanese bombers

[   ] line of defensive fortresses along France's border with Germany

[   ] U.S. president during World War II

[   ] Great Britain's prime minister during the Second World War

[   ] "lightning war" – German invasion of Poland

[   ] line of defensive fortresses along Germany's border with France

[   ] Spanish anti-Communists who fought in the Germany army

[   ] rich, grain-growing region in the USSR

[   ] Royal Air Force of Britain

[   ] alliance of Germany, Italy, and Japan

[   ] underground French resistance movement based in England

[   ] where Germany surrendered to the Allies after World War I and where France surrendered to Germany in World War II

19. *Answer the following. (pgs. 581 – 583)*

a. Why did many people in Soviet lands welcome Hitler's invasion of Russia?

_____

_____

b. What four countries in western Europe remained neutral during World War II? *(Hint: Check the map on pg. 581)*

_____   _____   _____   _____

c. What countries aided Russia in the war against Hitler? _____   _____

d. Fill in the blanks to explain why countries that were anti-Communist aided Stalin, a brutal Communist dictator:

"Any man or state who fights against _____ will have our _____. Any man or state who marches with _____ is our _____..."

e. What new enemies did Hitler make when he invaded Russia? _____

_____

f. How did the U.S. prepare for war in 1940? _____

_____

g. What did Great Britain and the U.S. do to try to defend the Philippines and stop Japanese aggression in the Pacific?

_____

_____

h. What did this provoke Japan to do? _____

_____

i. What event changed U.S. citizens' opposition to U.S. entry into World War II?

_____

j. What event happened on each of the following dates:

December 7, 1941 - _____

December 8, 1941 - _____

December 11, 1941 - _____

k. Give **two** ways U.S entry into the war changed the war:

* _____

   _____

* _____

   _____

Name _____ Date _____

Chapter 20: The End of a War and the Beginning of a New World

1. *Answer the following. (pgs. 589 – 591)*

a. What was one of the bloodiest and most destructive battles of World War II? _____

b. Who won the battle? _____

c. Why was it perhaps the most important battle of the war? _____

_____

_____

_____

_____

d. Where did the Allied forces begin their strike against Germany? _____

e. What did the Allies call their battle plan? _____

f. Who was the American general who led the Allied ground forces? _____

g. Write three decisions Roosevelt and Churchill made at their meeting in Casablanca:

- _____

- _____

- _____

h. Explain the plans for the Combined Bomber Offensive: _____

_____

_____

_____

i. What were the two goals of the Combined Bomber Offensive?

- _____

- _____

2. Fill in the blanks to complete this quote from President Roosevelt: *(pg. 591)*

"We do mean to impose _____ and _____ in full upon their guilty, _____ leaders."

3. *Number the events in the order they happened. (pgs. 591 – 593)*

a. _____ In October, the government of King Vittorio Emanuele formally declared war of Germany.

b. _____ On July 9, Allied planes dropped bombs on Rome.

c. _____ After their victory in North Africa, the Allies invaded Sicily and then moved on to the Italian peninsula.

d. _____ The Germans moved reinforcements into Italy.

e. _1_ On May 1943, General Rommel surrendered to the Allies in North Africa.

f. _____ The Fascist Grand Council asked King Vittorio Emanuele III to take control of the Italian government.

g. _____ On September 23, the Germans established the Italian Social Republic.

h. _____ The Allies finally pushed the Germans north and liberated Rome on June 4, 1944.

i. _____ King Vittorio forced Mussolini to resign as prime minister and had him arrested.

j. _____ Threatened by the German army, King Vittorio Emanuele fled from Rome.

k. _____ The new prime minister began secret peace negotiations with the Allies.

l. _8_ On September 3, the Italian government formally surrendered to the Allies.

m. _____ Hitler appointed Mussolini as prime minister of the Italian state completely under Hitler's control.

n. _____ For eight months, the Germans held back the Allied advance.

4. Write the details of the Conference at Teheran. *(pgs. 593 – 594)*

a. Date:	

b. Participants:

c. Topics of discussion:

d. Agreements made:

Did you know? The Conference of Teheran was held in the capital of Iran in the Middle East. Iran was neutral in the war but in 1941, Iran was invaded by British and Soviet forces. There were Germans living in Iran and that was given as an excuse for the invasion and the overthrow of the *shah* (king). The Allies wanted to secure the Iranian oil fields and keep the Allied supply lines open on the eastern front. The *shah* appealed to the U.S. for aid in stopping the invasion, but since the U.S. had not formally entered the war at that time, it would not help.

5. *Match the columns. (pgs. 594 – 595) A dictionary may be helpful.*

A. Holocaust

B. *Untermenschen*

C. *Kristallnacht*

D. *Einsatzgruppen*

E. Final Solution

F. ghetto

G. crematorium

H. euthanasia

[   ] furnace that burns dead bodies to ash

[   ] Hitler's decision to exterminate the Jewish race

[   ] painlessly killing a person who is suffering from an incurable illness or injury; also called "mercy" killing

[   ] a section of a city inhabited by a minority group

[   ] groups of armed men whose task was to kill Jews in German-occupied Territories

[   ] term referring to Hitler's attempts to exterminate the Jews; taken from the name of an Old Testament sacrifice that entirely destroyed its victim

[   ] "subhuman" - what Hitler called Jews

[   ] "Crystal Night" - night of November 8, 1938 when, throughout Germany, organized mobs burned down or damaged over 1,000 synagogues and broke the windows of over 7,500 Jewish businesses and ransacked them

6. *Answer the following. (pgs. 594 – 595)*

a. What other peoples did Hitler consider his enemies besides those he was fighting on the battlefield?

_____

_____

b. Who did Hitler consider his greatest enemy? _____

c. What kind of people did Hitler's government euthanize? _____

_____

d. Describe what happened to Jews sent to extermination camps, like Auschwitz in Poland:

_____

_____

_____

e. Describe what life was like in a concentration camp in Germany: _____

_____

_____

_____

f. What other people besides Jews suffered and died in these camps? _____

_____

g. How many people were estimated to have been murdered in the Holocaust? How many of these were Jewish?

_____

Did you know? Before Hitler settled on his "Final Solution," he mandated that Jews in the *Reich* wear something to distinguish them from other people when they were in public. Jews were required to wear a badge in the shape of a yellow, six-pointed star (the Jewish "Star of David"), sometimes with the word "Jew" written on it as well. It was a psychological tactic used to isolate and humiliate the Jews and any Jew who refused to wear the badge could be shot.

7. *In each statement below* <u>cross out</u> *the ending phrase that would make the statement false. (pgs. 595 – 597)*

a. Cardinal Eugenio Pacelli was…

> … the former papal nuncio to Germany under Pius XI.
>
> … elected pope shortly before the outbreak of World War II.
>
> … appointed pope by Pius XI before he died.
>
> … the Vatican Secretary of State under Pius XI.

b. During his reign, Pope Pius XII…

> … wrote an encyclical supporting the Allied efforts in the war.
>
> …. refused to take sides in the war.
>
> … continually called and worked for peace.
>
> … spoke out against the evils committed by both the Allies and the Axis.

c. Pope Pius XII condemned…

> … Hitler and the Nazis by name.
>
> … the persecution of peoples because of their race or nationality.
>
> … the bombing of cities, towns, and villages.
>
> … targeting noncombatant men, women, and children in the war.

d. Pius XII said the world was at war because…

> … it had rejected God and truth.
>
> … many countries did not have democratic governments.
>
> … mankind had embraced false ideas about God and man, such as Marxist socialism.
>
> … the Liberal economic system had oppressed workers and deprived them of justice and dignity.

e. Pope Pius XII did not speak out directly against the Holocaust in public because…

> … Jewish groups asked him not to do so.
>
> … public condemnations by religious leaders only pushed Hitler to further acts of cruelty.
>
> … it would have no effect on Hitler and would only make matters worse.
>
> … he did not really care what happened to the Jews.

f. Instead of making statements, Pius XII…

> … urged Catholic bishops not to get involved or harbor Jews.
>
> … provided many Jews false passports to escape the Nazi SS.
>
> … hid Jews at his summer residence, Castel Gandolfo, and in the Vatican City itself.
>
> … sent numerous diplomatic protests against anti-Jewish violence in Axis governments.

8. *Fill in the blanks. (pg. 597)*

a. It is estimated that _____ Jews escaped death at the hands of the Nazis because of the actions taken or encouraged by Pope Pius XII.

b. After the war, important _____ leaders praised Pope Pius XII and gave him the title of _____.

c. In 1967, Israeli historian, Pinchas Lapide, wrote:

> *"…Pius XII deserves that forest in the _____ which kindly people in _____ proposed for him in October 1958. A _____ forest… with _____ trees."*

9. *Number the events on the <u>western</u> front of the war in the order they happened. (pgs. 597 – 600)*

a. _____ The Allies broke through the German defensive line and crossed the Rhine.

b. _____ By mid-October, the Allies had taken the German city of Aachen.

c. _____ The Allies reach Berlin shortly after the Russians.

d. _____ In late January, the Allies resumed their advance to the Rhine.

e. _____ An Allied army liberated Luxemburg and crossed into Germany.

f. _____ The Germans put up a strong defense, but by July 24, they had been driven from Normandy.

g. _____ The Allies advanced toward Paris and on August 25, 1944, they liberated the city.

h. _1_ On June 6, 1944, British and American troops crossed the English Channel and began their invasion of France.

i. _____ As the German army was in full retreat, the Allies entered Belgium, taking Brussels and Antwerp.

j. _____ In December, the Germans desperately tried break the Allied lines, but were defeated at the Battle of the Bulge.

k. _____ To hinder the movement of German troops, the Allies began a bombing campaign over eastern German cities.

l. _____ The Allied air strikes weakened the German *Luftwaffe*, giving the Allies control of the skies.

l. _____ In November, the Allies advanced into the Saar region, but had trouble breaking through Germany's defensive Siegfried Line.

10. *Number the events on the <u>eastern</u> front of the war in the order they happened. (pgs. 597 – 600)*

a. _1_ After the Battle of Stalingrad, the Soviet Red Army began a steady advance against the Germans in the east.

b. _____ In five weeks, the Russians pushed the Germans entirely out of Ukraine and moved into Poland and Lithuania.

c. _____ In August 1943, the Red Army defeated the Germans at Kursk.

d. _____ The Red Army waited while the Nazis killed Polish patriots who had risen in revolt in the city.

e. _____ The German army retreated into Ukraine, and by the end of September had crossed the Dnieper River.

f. _____ By late July, the Red Army reached the outskirts of Warsaw and halted.

g. _____ Throughout the fall of 1943 and the winter of 1944, the Russians gradually pushed the Germans west.

h. _____ In June 1944, the Soviets opened an 800-mile front, from Leningrad to the Carpathian Mountains.

i. _____ In January 1945, the Russians began an invasion of Germany.

j. _____ In April, the Russian armies reached Berlin and began their attack of the city.

11. *Answer the following. (pgs. 597 – 600)*

a. What was the code name for the Allied invasion of France? _____

b. Who was the American general who commanded the invasion? _____

c. Write two advantages the Soviet Red Army had over the Germans by 1943:

- _____

- _____

d. Why did even Germans who hated Hitler fiercely resist the Allied invasion of their country?

_____

_____

_____

12. *Circle the word or phrase in bold to complete each sentence. (pgs. 599 – 600)*

a. While the invasions of Germany were going on, Roosevelt, Churchill, and Stalin met at **[Yalta/ Dresden]**. on the Black Sea to discuss **[what to do with Hitler when he was captured/ the future of Europe after the war]**.

b. Stalin was given an important role in the decision-making because he had become **[indispensable/ superfluous]** to the Allied war effort.

c. Because Roosevelt and Churchill **[did not need/ needed]** Stalin as an ally, they **[refused/ gave in to]** his demands.

c. Great Britain and Stalin decided to split **[Yugoslavia and Hungary/ Greece and Italy]** between them.

d. Stalin was allowed to form a new government for **[Germany/ Poland]** if he promised to **[crush the Nazi party/ respect democracy and free elections]**.

e. Stalin also was given the right to use forced **[German/Polish]** labor **[indefinitely/ for 10 years]**.

f. The Allies agreed to divide Germany into **[four zones/ two countries]**, each controlled by an Allied power.

g. Roosevelt and Churchill were **[satisfied/ not happy]** with the results of the Yalta conference and were **[praised/ criticized]** for its outcome.

13. After the Soviets reached Berlin, the war quickly came to an end. *Write what happened on these dates. (pg. 600)*

a. April 28, 1945 in Berlin: _____

b. April 28, 1945 in Italy: _____

c. April 30, 1945 in Berlin: _____

d. By May 4, 1945: _____

e. May 8, 1945: _____

14. Write **four** devastating effects of World War II on Europe: *(pg. 601)*

- _____
  _____

- _____
  _____

- _____
  _____

- _____
  _____

15. What historical process did World War I begin and World War II complete? *(pg. 601)*

_____
_____
_____
_____

Name _____ Date _____

16. *Fill in the blanks. (pgs. 601 – 602)*

a. President Roosevelt hoped the United Nations Organization would act like a world _____ of

nations and assure _____ and _____ to all peoples everywhere.

b. The charter for the United Nations was approved in _____ in October 1945.

c. The United Nations is divided into two bodies: the _____ Council and the _____ .

d. The "Big Five" nations - the United States, _____, _____, _____,

and _____ - sit on the _____ Council.

e. The remaining member nations send _____ to the _____ and each nation gets

_____ vote.

f. The _____ must approve all resolutions and any of the five members can _____

a resolution.

g. The UN has the power to approve the use of _____ (_____ sanctions and even _____)

against nations that oppose its decrees.

h. The UN can establish its own permanent _____ .

i. Because the _____ dominates it, the full force of the UN can never be used against any

of the _____ or any of their interests.

Did you know? The chief administrator and spokesperson for the United Nations is called the
Secretary-General. The Secretary-General is appointed by the member nations and the position is
usually held for a five-year term. Find out who the current Secretary-General is and what country
he/she comes from: _____

17. *The map below shows how Germany and Austria were carved up by the <u>United States</u>, <u>Great Britain</u>, <u>France</u> and
the <u>USSR</u>. Using the descriptions on pg. 603 in the textbook, label what country occupied each section.*

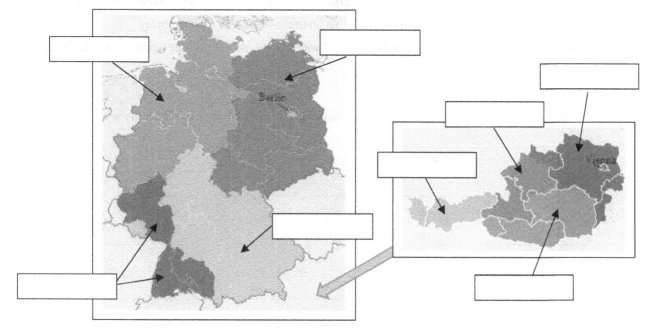

18. *Compete the following. (pgs. 602 – 604)*

a. Circle the countries that had Communist governments after World War II:

> Albania   Austria   Bulgaria   Czechoslovakia   eastern Germany   France   Hungary
>
> Italy   Poland   Romania   western Germany   Yugoslavia

b. Why did the countries your circled become Communist? _____

_____

_____

c. What country overthrew its monarchy and became a republic after the war? _____

d. After the occupation of Germany, the Allied nations stopped cooperating with one another. Check the reasons why:

_____ France would do nothing to help Germany recover and rebuild.

_____ Great Britain wanted to starve the German people to keep them weak.

_____ France wanted to annex Germany's industrial regions.

_____ The Soviets did not deliver promised food to the western sectors of Germany.

_____ The U.S. and Great Britain had to pay for food shipments to Germany out of their own government funds.

_____ France was gutting eastern German's industry.

_____ The western Allies stopped reparation payments from their sectors to the Soviets.

_____ The United States would not allow the Germans to set up their own governments.

_____ Stalin broke the promises he had made at the Yalta conference.

e. What did the Western democratic nations think was the new threat to freedom in the world? _____

19. *Match the columns. (pgs. 603 – 604)*

A. denazification   [   ] hostility that developed between Western democracies and the Soviet Union

B. Nuremberg Trials   [   ] line of division between democratic nations and Communist nations

C. Truman Doctrine   [   ] tribunals in Bavaria that tried Nazis accused of war crimes and other atrocities

D. Cold War   [   ] attempt to stamp out all traces of Nazism from Germany

E. Iron Curtain   [   ] the U.S. would stand with free peoples all over the world against the threat of oppression

19. *Answer the following. (pgs. 604 – 605)*

a. Write **five** ways the United States helped the postwar nations of Western Europe rebuild after the war:

- _____

- _____

- _____

- _____

- _____

b. What trouble hit Europe in 1947? _____

c. Why was this event perilous for Europe? _____

_____

_____

Name _____ Date _____

d. Explain President Truman's "Marshall Plan" to help Europe: _____

_____

_____

_____

_____

_____

e. What countries rejected U.S. aid? _____

f. The U.S. Congress was hesitant to support the Marshall Plan. What event convinced them to approve it?

_____

_____

g. What were the results of the Marshall Plan on Europe? _____

_____

_____

_____

h. What was the only Western European country that did not at first benefit from the Marshall Plan? _____

20. *Number the events in the order they happened. (pgs. 605 – 606)*

a. _____ In June 1948, the Soviets blocked all shipments of food and supplies to Western-controlled sectors of Berlin.

b. _____ A new constitution was written for the newly-formed West Germany.

c. _____ In response to the formation of West Germany, the Soviets formed the state of East Germany.

d. _____ France, Great Britain, and the U.S. merged their sectors of occupied Germany to form a united German state.

e. _____ Great Britain, France, and the U.S. began airlifting supplies into western Berlin.

f. __1__ The U.S., Great Britain, and France issued a new currency for Germany.

g. _____ West Germany received aid from the Marshall Plan and began to experience economic recovery.

h. _____ The Soviets protested this move, saying it was done without consulting them.

i. _____ Stalin called off the Berlin blockade in May 1949.

j. _____ West Germany became a full sovereign state and a member of NATO in 1955.

k. _____ The U.S. and eleven Europe nations signed the North Atlantic Treaty, in which they pledged to come to each other's aid in the event of war.

21. *Answer the following. (pg. 606)*

a. What eleven European nations signed the North Atlantic Treaty with the U.S.? _____

_____

b. What does NATO stand for? _____

c. What kind of government did East Germany have and who controlled it? _____

_____

22. *Match the columns. (pgs. 605 – 607)*

A. NATO

B. currency

C. Deutsche Mark

D. Federal Republic of Germany

E. German Democratic Republic

F. Berlin Wall

G. Anti-Fascist Protection Wall

H. Wall of Shame

I. Warsaw Pact

J. November 1989

K. October 3, 1990

L. March 1994

M. United States

N. Soviet Union

[　] Berlin reestablished as the capital of a united Germany

[　] what the East German government called the Berlin Wall

[　] East Germany

[　] beginning of the demolition of the Berlin Wall

[　] superpower of the Western bloc

[　] Germany currency, established in 1948

[　] superpower of the Eastern bloc

[　] reunification of East and West Germany

[　] defense organization of free nations against Soviet aggression

[　] Money in actual use in a country

[　] West Germany

[　] barrier erected in 1961 to keep East Germans from escaping to West Berlin

[　] what Germans in West Berlin called the Berlin Wall

[　] defense alliance between the Soviet Union and other Communist states in Europe

23. *Answer the following. (pg. 608)*

a. What was the "Manhattan Project"? _____

_____

_____

b. What country dropped the first atomic bomb? _____

c. When was it dropped? _____

d. What city was bombed? _____

e. What city was bombed three days later? _____

f. What was the effect on the bombed cities? _____

_____

_____

_____

g. What did President Truman call the atomic bomb? _____

Did you know? Nuclear physicist J. Robert Oppenheimer directed the development of the atomic bomb for the United States. Security was very tight at the development sites and most employees did not know exactly what they were working on. The bomb was so top secret that the public was not informed about the 1945 test explosion in the New Mexico desert, despite the radioactive danger. US. citizens did not know their country had such destructive weapons until the bombing of Japan was reported in the news.

24. *In each statement below <u>cross out</u> the ending phrase that would make the statement false. (pgs. 608 – 609)*

a. Dropping the atomic bombs on Japan …

> … caused Japan to surrender, ending World War II in the Pacific.
>
> … unleashed a destructive power beyond the worst dreams of mankind.
>
> … created a new world problem.
>
> … was in accord with Catholic just war principles.

b. The Acheson-Lilienthal Report of 1946 …

> … was drawn up by the United Nations Atomic Energy Commission.
>
> … said that atomic research should be used for peaceful development of nations rather than war.
>
> … advised that an international authority own the plutonium and uranium used to produce atomic energy.
>
> … advised that an international authority own the reactors and facilities used in atomic energy production.

c. U.S. President Truman…

> … did not want the U.S. to give up its atomic weapons or raw materials.
>
> … wanted an international authority only to inspect a country's atomic weapons and stockpiles.
>
> … sent the original Acheson-Lilienthal Report to the UN Atomic Energy Commission.
>
> … rejected the Soviet proposal to dismantle all atomic arsenals.

d. Four years after the first atomic bomb was dropped…

> … the UN Atomic Energy Commission was still discussing what to do with atomic energy.
>
> … China successfully tested its first atomic bomb.
>
> … the U.S. continued to produce atomic weaponry.
>
> … the Soviet Union successfully tested its first atomic bomb.

e. In China, Mao Tse-Tung…

> … came to power when the Communist Party won the 1949 Chinese election.
>
> … established a Communist regime called the People's Republic of China.
>
> … expelled all Western missionaries and persecuted religious believers.
>
> … allied himself with Stalin.

25. *Complete the following. (pgs. 609 – 612)*

a. <u>Check</u> the statements that describe Western Europe in the late 1940s and the 1950s:

_____ Most of the nations recovered from the war and experienced economic prosperity.

_____ European nations granted independence to most of their overseas colonies.

_____ Socialism and Communism became unpopular.

_____ Western Europe fully embraced *laissez-faire* capitalism.

_____ Governments worked with unions and business owners to create systems to protect workers' rights.

_____ Governments established state-run insurance to provide inexpensive or free medical aid to all citizens.

_____ Western Europe develop a system of government called social democracy.

_____ The war had erased all tensions and rivalries between European nations.

b. Write two things the U.S. thought Western European nations needed to keep from becoming Communist:

- _____

- _____

c. Fill in the blanks to complete the steps to a more united Europe.

- The European _____ was established to make sure all members could easily _____ with each other and that the European industries could _____ with industries from outside Europe.

- The European _____ was founded to assure that no one member country could hoard _____ or _____ from other members.

- In 1957, Belgium, France, West Germany, Italy, Luxembourg, and the Netherlands, formed the European _____ which removed trade _____ between member countries and set up _____to protect the EEC from cheap goods _____ from other countries.

- In 1993, the _____ was founded. It serves as a kind of _____ government for the independent member nations.

d. Where did the center of world culture move after World War II? _____

e. Write **five** statements to describe America in the 1950s:

- _____
  _____

- _____
  _____

- _____
  _____

- _____
  _____

- _____
  _____

f. Write **four** ways European culture became Americanized:

- _____
- _____
- _____
- _____

g. What became the symbol of America for many Europeans? _____

h. What term was coined to refer to the influence of American mass culture in Europe? _____

i. Write **three** negative effects of the spread of American culture throughout the world:

- _____
- _____
- _____

Name _____ Date _____

j. Explain why Communist ideas, revolts, and governments spread throughout the world as Western economic practices spread:

_____

_____

_____

_____

26. *In each statement below* <u>cross out</u> *the ending phrase that would make the statement false. (pgs. 613 – 614)*

a. The Church's problem with the modern world was that…

      … its basic ideas were based on Liberalism.
      … it said personal happiness was the only purpose of life.
      … its scientific discoveries contradicted the Bible.
      … it said that religion had no place in the real world.

b. The Church tried to deal with the modern world by…

      … sorting out the truths mixed up with the errors of Liberalism.
      … condemning human reason and science.
      … offering a Catholic alternative to the problems with capitalism and socialism.
      … seeking out the best way to apply the ancient teachings of the Faith to the modern world.

c. The post-World War II world was rapidly changing because…

      … millions of people were leaving the cities and moving to the suburbs.
      … new discoveries and inventions were giving men unimaginable power over nature.
      … old agrarian societies were being destroyed.
      … people were losing touch with ancient traditions of thinking and behaving.

d. After World War II more and more people were abandoning religion because…

      … they put their hopes in science and technology instead of Christ.
      … they were pursuing wealth and the comforts that go with it.
      … they were striving to create their heaven on Earth instead of preparing themselves for heaven.
      … the Church taught that science was contrary to religion.

e. Pope John XXIII called the Second Vatican Council because…

      … he thought the Church should change some of its doctrines and teachings.
      … he wanted to find new ways the Church could spread the Gospel to the modern world.
      … he wanted the Church to look to future times without fear.
      … he thought the Church needed to be refreshed and updated.

f. The Second Vatican Council…

      … called for dialogue with non-Catholic Christians and people of other religions.
      … called for a renewal of worship by making the Mass more comprehensible to modern people.
      … discussed the ways the Church can speak to and work with people of the modern world.
      … changed the teachings on the nature of the Church and her Sacraments.

27. What was the one great goal of the Second Vatican Council? *(pg. 615)*

_____

_____

_____

28. *Answer the following. (pg. 616)*

a. In its document *Dignitatis Humanae,* what did the Second Vatican's Counci call for?

_____

b. Why did this surprise many and seem to contradict traditional Catholic teaching on the relation of Church and state?

_____

_____

_____

_____

c. Explain how *Dignitatis Humanae* does not contradict traditional Church teaching:

_____

_____

_____

_____

_____

_____

_____

_____

d. Explain how the Council's reason for calling for the same thing is different than the Liberals' reason:

_____

_____

_____

_____

29. *Complete the following. (pgs. 615 – 617)*

a. After the Second Vatican Council, Catholics all over the world began to think that the Church had undergone a radical revolution. <u>Check</u> the true reasons why Catholics thought this:

_____ Secular newspapers daily reported deep divisions between "liberal" and "conservative" council fathers.

_____ Pope John XXIII urged the council fathers to make changes to church teachings.

_____ The rite of the Mass that had been offered for centuries was drastically changed.

_____ New music for Mass did not sound like traditional sacred music.

_____ Many Catholic theologians said that the Church had changed and was a new Church.

_____ The Second Vatican Council's documents proposed major changes of Church doctrines.

_____ Dissenting theologians were not punished by their bishops or the Holy See.

_____ Many theologians said Catholics had to follow their own consciences rather than Church authority.

_____ After the council, Pope Paul VI taught different teachings than his predecessors.

_____ It seemed like the Church was trying to be more like the modern world.

b. Write **four** ways Catholics were affected by the belief that the Church was not the same as it had been:

- _____
- _____
- _____
- _____

c. In 1962, what did Pope John XXIII say would happen if all Catholics put the teachings of Vatican II into effect? Complete the quote:

"...then, without doubt, shall shine forth the desired new _____, which will more abundantly _____ the Church with _____ powers and shall spread her maternal, inspired, and saving power through all the spheres of _____."

d. Ten years later, what was Pope Paul VI's comment on the aftermath of the council? Complete the quote:

"It was believed that after the council, there would come a _____ in the history of the Church, but instead there came a day of _____, _____ and _____ ... By some crack, the smoke of _____ has entered the _____."

30. Despite the increasing problems in the world and in the Church, Catholics are continually called to renew both the world and the Church. What two virtues, as exemplified by Pius IX and John XXIII, should inspire Catholics as they try to do this? Explain how Catholics can influence history by practicing these two virtues. *(pgs. 617 – 620)*

_____

_____

_____

_____

_____

_____

_____

_____